THE POWER OF STRATEGIC COMMITMENT

Kelly —

Great working together!

Josh Leibner

THE POWER OF STRATEGIC COMMITMENT

Achieving Extraordinary Results Through
Total Alignment and Engagement

Josh Leibner
Gershon Mader
Alan Weiss, Ph.D.

AMACOM

American Management Association

New York * Atlanta * Brussels * Chicago * Mexico City * San Francisco
Shanghai * Tokyo * Toronto * Washington, D. C.

Special discounts on bulk quantities of AMACOM books are available to corporations, professional associations, and other organizations. For details, contact Special Sales Department, AMACOM, a division of American Management Association, 1601 Broadway, New York, NY 10019. Tel: 212-903-8316. Fax: 212-903-8083.
E-mail: specialsls@amanet.org
Website: www.amacombooks.org/go/specialsales
To view all AMACOM titles go to: www.amacombooks.org

This publication is designed to provide accurate and authoritative information in regard to the subject matter covered. It is sold with the understanding that the publisher is not engaged in rendering legal, accounting, or other professional service. If legal advice or other expert assistance is required, the services of a competent professional person should be sought.

"Strategic Commitment" is a registered service mark of Quantum Performance, Inc.

Library of Congress Cataloging-in-Publication Data

Leibner, Josh.
    The power of strategic commitment : achieving extraordinary results through total alignment and engagement / Josh Leibner, Gershon Mader, Alan Weiss.
      p.cm.
    Includes index.
    ISBN 978-0-8144-1374-6 (HC)   ISBN 978-0-8144-3440-6 (PB)
    1. Organizational effectiveness. 2. Strategic planning. 3. Management. I. Mader, Gershon. II. Weiss, Alan, 1946– III. Title.
    HD58.9.L545 2009
    658.4'012—dc22
                                                                                            2009004734

Printing number
10 9 8 7 6 5 4 3 2 1

For Sammy—in my heart, always and forever. Mom, Laurie and Shoshana—thank you for your love and support. Dad, you would have enjoyed the read.

—Josh

For Na'ama, Ongi, Eden, and Osher, thank you for your unwavering love and support.

—Gershon

For Maria and another wonderful forty years . . .

—Alan

CONTENTS

Chapter 10: Strategic Commitment as Organizational Lifestyle   181

Integrating the Process into Organizational DNA

Chapter 11: The Diversity of Strategic Commitment   203

There Is No Such Thing as "But We're Different"

Afterword: Strategic Commitment Is Essential in Volatile Economies

Appendix: Tips, Techniques, and Tools for Generating, Monitoring, and Addressing Setbacks Related to Strategic Commitment

ACKNOWLEDGMENTS

There are many who have contributed to our thinking around Strategic Commitment and helped make this book possible. Some we have studied with closely; others we know through their writings. Some have been partners in our efforts, and many, through their trust and generosity, have allowed us to do what we love most: contribute to their personal leadership style and their organizations' growth.

Our thanks to Larry Bossidy and Ram Charan for their manifesto on execution; Joel Barker for the pioneering work on paradigms; Jim Collins for distinguishing the great from the good; Werner Erhard for breaking new ground in thinking about transformation; Fernando Flores for the relationship between language and action; Gary Hamel for strategic intent; Henry Mintzberg for his deep understanding that strategy alone is insufficient; Richard Pascale for managing on the edge; Charles Savage for his insights about organizational culture and behavior; Peter Senge for enrollment; Charles Smith for a new way to think about the future; and Dan Sullivan for teaching entrepreneurship.

The development of Strategic Commitment would not have been possible without those with whom we have worked. It is not practical to mention everyone by name, even though many have become friends along the way. Therefore we would like to thank the following leaders, and their team members, who are not mentioned here:

Edison Peres, Marilyn Miller, Keith Goodwin, Mike Allen, Jim Anderson, Andreas Dohmen, Thierry Drilhon, Duncan Mitchell, Phil Smith, John Donovan, Charlie Johnston, Gordon Thomson, Mark Hamberlin, Andrew Sage, Surinder Brarr, Mark Bonfoy, Liz Lawson, Alex Thurber, Sharon Bachar, Danielle Shany, Boaz Maoz, Tony Marano, Jim Costigan, Bruce Mosler, John Santora, Maureen Waters, Chris Lowrey, Joe Harbert, the C&W NYC Metro Region Brokers and teams, Frank Liantonio, Marc Renard, Colum Bastable, Pierre Bergevin, Mark Wanic, Carolyn Sessa, John Parro, Lori Doyle, Claudia Grandjean, Roberto Gregory, Horst Peterson, Dave Mezzanotte, Al Trujillo, Elise Glennon, Mike Moynahan, Erez Weinrach, Margit Elo, Stephen Berstein, Steve Linehan, Gary Perlin, Rob Alexander, Lynn Pike, Mike Zamsky, Jack Forestell, David Hummelberg, Frank LaPrade, John Powenski, Jeff O'Dell, Steve Rand, Robert Landry, Ron Mayer, Ken Berger, David Siesko, John Weaver, Jack Reynolds, Helen Galt, Jim White, Tome Swanekamp, Andrew Maggion, Sarah Kiyingi-Kaweesa, Susan Lubega, Monica Anton, and Finbarr Flood.

Thanks also to our good friends Terry Rosenberg and Tony Freedley for their friendship and guidance; to Steve Linehan for his thoughts on leadership; and to Leslie Tucker for guiding John Weaver to "Top 10."

We also want to especially thank Bob Buday for supporting us in figuring out who we are.

Last, Alan Weiss—thank you for your partnership, wisdom, and friendship.

Josh Leibner

Gershon Mader

* * *

My thanks to Art Strohmer, formerly at Merck, and Marilyn Martiny, formerly at Hewlett-Packard, for helping me become a decent consultant: If I only knew then what I know now, but we did fine, didn't we?!

Alan Weiss

INTRODUCTION

Let's be honest. Most initiatives to improve organizational performance do not deliver. Whether the aim is to become leaner, more productive, customer-intimate, or growth-oriented, the majority of organizational programs fail to accomplish their goals. Most of these efforts don't cut costs, improve productivity, boost customer satisfaction, or raise revenue to the levels that the organization's leaders expected or promised to the board and Wall Street. Some initiatives, in fact, fail outright because of lack of ownership and follow-through. All in all, the track record of corporate initiatives is a sorry one—one that only Dilbert creator Scott Adams could take joy in.

Most senior managers understand that no matter how clear and valid their strategy and objectives are, if people are not genuinely on the same page working with each other, rather than against or independent of each other, they will not achieve the success they want. But these same managers don't know *how* to generate real commitment and alignment to their strategies. One clear indication is the lack of enthusiasm that most senior managers exhibit for the strategic planning process. As one executive put it, "Strategic planning—that's when you go offsite as a team, agree on a bunch of priorities for the year, then go back to work and do what you were going to do anyway."

From our combined consulting experience spanning eighty-plus years, 500 clients, and sixty countries, working with companies of all types and at all levels, we have found that the root cause for most failed or unfulfilled strategies is not any actual shortcomings in the strategies themselves. In fact, we have seen brilliant strategies fail in the worst way—despite being *exactly* what the company needed at the time, well researched and analyzed, and presented compellingly at all levels.

The Power of Strategic Commitment teaches how true ownership and commitment, and not merely compliance, is achieved throughout an organization, even when the environment is filled with the typical toxic organizational issues of distrust, politics, turfism, butt-covering, blame, and timidity. The book addresses the role, for example, of a "chief commitment officer," ways to build commitment that cost nothing, and the fallacy of money as a motivator for behavior change. Strategic commitment issues in nonprofits, education, and government, as well as traditional for-profits, are all covered.

Using this book, you'll be able to identify apathy, resignation, and cynicism, and then transform them into an environment of total alignment and commitment within your organization. The process starts by sharpening your antennae to spot compliance masquerading as commitment, and understanding the six key drivers that ensure organizational commitment, even under the most dire of circumstances. Numerous real-life examples are given from Global 1000 executives who have succeeded using these tools. All of the quotes used in the book come from direct interviews or interactions with clients, or recollections from the individuals cited. Actual names were used when possible, with fictionalized names used in some cases.

This book is a modest insurance policy to guarantee that the $400,000 spent on strategic planning is, indeed, well spent.

Please note: Beginning with *In Search of Excellence* almost 30 years ago (1982, HarperCollins), people have carped that companies used as examples have often fallen out of favor. That's because Peters and Waterman at the time, just as we are today, were using contemporary examples of sound processes. But variables often interfere: changed leadership, mergers, poor decisions, poor discipline, etc. We can't ensure that our examples will stay true to strategic commitment, but we can laud those that were doing so when we wrote this.

—Josh Leibner
Bridgewater, New Jersey

—Gershon Mader
Toronto, Ontario

—Alan Weiss
East Greenwich, Rhode Island
December 2008

THE POWER OF STRATEGIC COMMITMENT

◆ ◆ ◆

CHAPTER 1

WHY COMMITMENT TRUMPS COMPLIANCE

Why Commitment Is More Important Than Ever

The attainment of strategic goals is the lifeblood of any organization. Whether for-profit, nonprofit, local, global, large, small, service, or manufacturing, entities will drift, decline, and die if they aren't in pursuit of a managed, intelligent future.

Ideally, every employee should be acting in concert with that future—the strategic goals of the organization. The larger the organization, the more important it is because there is more chance of people going astray. Think of an athletic team where a third of the players aren't executing on the plays called to score. That's impossible in match play golf, improbable but possible in doubles tennis, and sometimes glaringly obvious in football or soccer.

That's why *commitment*—the innate willingness of people to follow and contribute—always trumps *compliance*—the forced adherence to plans created through manipulation, punishment, and coercion.

Even the Most Successful Organizations Don't Operate at Their Full Potential

Our unequivocal experience on a global basis is that leaders do not believe that their organizations are performing anywhere near their full potential (never mind "raising the bar"). Before you write that notion off because you think good leaders always demand a "stretch" from their people while bad leaders always demand mindless growth, consider these factors.

First, business is more complex today than ever before, and it is growing still more complex by the hour. One prognostication that always sounds sage and is universally safe is that "the rate of change is increasing." It is difficult to perform within some optimal range when we realize that "optimal" is a moving target. With the notable exception of the postal service, which simply can demand that its customers suffer through lower standards of performance and pay ever-increasing rates, nearly every enterprise finds itself dealing with the complexity of demanding higher performance.

The competition has demanded that cable TV provide narrower service commitments that are accurately fulfilled; that cell phones become smaller and cheaper while accommodating more features; that first-class international carriers provide flat beds and even private suites; and that movie theaters show athletic events and music concerts because the Internet and cable are such powerful competitors for classic theatrical entertainment.

Second, agility and responsiveness are now among the most important qualities for any organization. Online purchasing has created a new legion of buyers who aren't willing to wait for bored salespeople to attend to them in retail outlets. Yet Apple, Inc. was able to create very successful retail outlets by assigning a salesperson to customers from their moment of entry, through all purchases, right up to departures. (As one woman shopper was heard to remark, "Life should be like this, with a man assigned to you for as long as you want him.")

People want frontline personnel at the hotel desk, the bank window, or the reservations line to take care of problems, obstacles, and special requests. That's true agility. They don't want to wait for managers, policy reviews, and return calls. That's sorry ossification.

Third, Tom Friedman is absolutely accurate in his assessment of the world being flat. Someone from the United Kingdom contributing to one of our international chat rooms was asked how he could be present and take part in a dozen or more different discussions each day. "It's easy," he explained, "I outsource 75 percent of my responses to India."

That outsourcing has become a comic metaphor is critical to understanding why true commitment is so important. Boeing is having trouble with its next-generation airplane, the 787 Dreamliner, because of sourcing problems from halfway around the world. A Bentley, assembled in Crewe, England, is basically German engineering, owned by Volkswagen but controlled by Porsche. Cash in frequent-flyer miles on any U.S. carrier and you have a better than even chance of speaking to someone in the Philippines. Our point is that some "glue," some adhesion, is required to create common focus and rally energy behind initiatives in organizations whose parts are literally spread all over the globe.

Fourth, matrix management is growing more common *externally*, not just internally (where it causes enough problems and complexity). Employees report to a multiplicity of functions and superiors in multiple locations. How do leaders seamlessly set objectives, meet objectives, and galvanize people to action who may have conflicting interests within the matrix?

Hewlett-Packard is a wonderful case in point. You can be speaking to someone in Mountain View, California, who reports to someone in Brussels, who has three top aides in Boston, but who reports into a unit in Hong Kong. These people rarely see each other in person, but that may all change because of a marvelous new technology called the "virtual office." Being able to interact with someone virtually in the room, someone who is actually antipodally distant, creates those new levels of "optimal performance" we alluded to previously. The more organizations engage in matrix-like structures, with people reporting to multiple superiors (who may have different and even competing interests), the more important it is for a common strategic commitment to accentuate common objectives and goals for these diverse relationships.

Fifth, hold onto your hat, but the customer has more choices than ever. *And customers want to reduce their complexity while the seller or provider is experiencing increased complexity.*

It is tougher than ever for consumers to make purchase decisions because there are too many options among flat-screen TVs, or cell phones, or investment alternatives, or timeshare vacations. One way to reduce complexity is for customers to seek out

> **StratComment**
> *The inherent conflict and paradox, between organizations forced to deal with greater complexity and customers who crave minimal complexity, is one of the most significant demands for increased commitment facing organizations today.*

trusting, loyal, and valued relationships, which tend to be immune from price comparison and commodity thinking. In other words, if I can trust you to choose my product or service, you've reduced my complexity and I'm willing to pay more for that. Trust is encouraged in a myriad of business areas when strategic commitment creates two dynamics: 1) fewer choices because of clear goals and 2) the trust in others generated by the agreement on common goals, thus enabling delegated and shared decision making.

Of course, that increases the organization's complexity, in having to provide "ideal" solutions for diverse, global customers. That's why we may find some companies competing in one geographic area but collaborating in others (e.g., airline code sharing), and why mergers and acquisitions are growing rapidly to try to provide greater options, even though the great preponderance of them fail within three years. (This seems to stun many observers and even consultants, but it's never surprised us because we believe many executives who understand the theory of "scale, integration, and maximizing synergies" don't actually understand how to engage people to fully own, implement, and internalize those synergies in real life.)

Sixth, and finally, through this entire minefield there is one great constant: people. No matter how complex and sophisticated the landscape, success is, more than ever, a function of how people interact, collaborate, communicate, and respond. These are all fundamental attributes of successful execution, which is what distinguishes the good from the great, the winners from the losers.

Thus, operating at "full potential" is a bit of an oxymoron because once attained, we would make the point that it is no longer "full potential." For some years, books have been written on "execution" and "motivation" and "leadership." The reason that they are provocative is that they deal with one or more of the factors we have detailed. But these books could provide even greater impact if they provided executives significantly deeper insight into how to more fully engage their organizations. Given all of these factors, that engagement is more urgently needed today than ever.

It's a Question of Now or Never

Many organizations are locked into "causes" and "missions" that feature differences without a distinction: shareholder value, customer-driven value, just-in-time service—you name it. Yet they tend to miss the most important true difference in their potential improvement of performance and culture—namely, that *commitment is entirely distinct from compliance*. It is no semantic accident that government regulatory demands are called "compliance" factors and that consultants who assist in meeting such regulations are compliance consultants. No one in our experience has ever called them "commitment audits" or "commitment violations." They are nonvoluntary, often bureaucratic, and usually resented.

Even the most sophisticated organizations, with well-defined systems and processes, find that their most brilliant initiatives are frequently implemented very poorly. (Ram Charan and Larry Bossidy wrote an entire book on the subject, *Execution*.) Our firsthand observations over many years and working with many organizations are consistent and clear: When strategy fails it is almost always due to poor implementation, not poor formulation.

Why is it that so many leaders and lead-ing firms can spend hundreds of thousands of dollars on creating strategy (often hiring expensive external consultants, scheduling lush retreats, and paying many months of salary and benefits) and end up with a con-sensus strategy that is completely bollixed a year later?

> **StratComment**
>
> *Consensus is not com-mitment. People agree to "live with" something, but that doesn't mean they would "die for" it. Often, they simply want to get the meeting over with and return to work or go home.*

Unsurprisingly, managers are more loyal to personal agendas and interests, for which they possess true, sin-cere, and undying commitment! They are all too ready to comply with someone else's agenda as long as they can fulfill the commit-ment to their own.

In Margaret Thatcher's memoir, *The Downing Street Years*, Forbes Burnham, the one-time president of Guyana, defines consensus as "something you have if you cannot get agreement." Thatcher en-larged the definition:

> To me consensus seems to be: the process of abandoning all be-liefs, principles, values, and policies in search of something in which no one believes, but to which no one objects; the process of avoiding the very issues that have to be solved, merely be-cause you cannot get agreement on the way ahead. What great cause would have been fought for and won under the banner "I stand for consensus"?

So the choice of protecting one's turf, preserving resources, safe-guarding their advancement potential, and generally ameliorating their workload overwhelm superiors' expectations that they will en-thusiastically support initiatives that may conflict with these values. (A very effective promotional technique in conservative organiza-tions with which we have worked is to "stay off the radar screen" or "don't rock the boat." That is, it's a faster track to promotion *not* to be visible in great victories or great defeats than it is to be a constant target of attention. You can call this "blipless career progression.")

In unguarded and off-the-record moments, many executives have revealed to us that corporate politics are a *primary* factor in their decision making. Politics often influence decisions and can readily unhorse the lead rider trying to organize a charge toward strategic goals. At this writing, Bob Nardelli's difficulty with the board of The Home Depot is clearly a primary example, as was Hewlett-Packard and its board during Carly Fiorina's reign. And while you may encounter a tough negotiating position by pilots at FedEx, or huge debates about open architecture at Apple, you don't find internal politics disrupting organizational direction.

The converse is that we have been shocked yet eventually have grown accustomed (but still somewhat surprised every time) to organizations that have adequate (at best) processes and systems, but thrive through rapid obtainment of strategic goals because of incredibly high levels of internal alignment, ownership of initiatives, and accountability. Southwest Airlines develops huge commitment every day, right down to the frontline, and is consequently able to remain light on its feet and make quick changes as the market demands, with minimal disruption to operations and customers and thereby with minimal cost.

If you have the time and inexplicable desire to track the statistics on these things at The Conference Board, the American Management Association, or the archives of *The Wall Street Journal*, you'll find that upwards of 80 percent of mergers and acquisitions fail. We don't say that lightly—we mean "fail." (Our definition of failure is that the strategic goals that justified the merger or buyout were simply not met within the expected time frame. In many cases, the resultant organization was less effective and less successful than the original two by themselves, and in the extreme, the merged parties considered abandoning their plans in the hopes of producing increased shareholder value as separate entities. AOL/Time Warner is a classic example.)

One of the grandest examples was Daimler-Benz's takeover of Chrysler. It was doomed from the beginning because of the disingenuous claim that it was a "merger" even as the German executives were bragging of their "purchase." Virtually no one outside the Daimler boardroom was committed to this monstrosity, and it failed in breathtaking time, damaging customers, employees, and, of course, shareholders.

They may get it right "on paper" (sensible processes and systems, integration plans, and all the rest of the PowerPoint presentation), but these combinations still don't deliver what they promise. That's because the organizations can't "integrate" the hearts and minds of their people with slide projectors or pie charts. They fail to include (and many times, even consider) how to embrace people in the process and take two different cultures and identities and transform them into a new entity that is stronger than either of its components.

If one plus one doesn't equal at least 122 in these recombinations, they are not worth doing.

We once consulted with a huge insurance firm that had "devoured" a partner of almost equal size. We were asked for a communications strategy for the new entity, yet the senior team did not have any idea which offices would be closed, which executives would be retained, which benefits programs would prevail, and so on.

"You don't need a communications strategy," we told them, "since you have no idea of what you want to say. But you'd better start listening to people this afternoon and embracing them in your strategic intent." The executives were simply shocked to hear our recommendation, but they quickly came around when some top talent chose to depart the company rather than wait for another shoe to drop.

Most leaders try to "fix" declines in productivity and performance (revenue, profitability, quality, customer satisfaction, and so forth) by "reengineering" their processes. This is sometimes needed, but it is insufficient in and of itself to correct the situation.

In the early 1990s, process reengineering, thanks to Michael Hammer, et al., was *the* most popular organizational business response to improve effectiveness at all operational levels. By the late 1990s, it had become apparent that you could improve processes until the cows came home, but if people and functions were not genuinely on board and buying in, then productivity gains would be ephemeral at best. Around this time, we were competing with Ernst and Young for a consulting contract at Hewlett-Packard. Ernst and Young had just finished a huge reengineering process, and the Ernst partner suggested that HP could apply "templates" to bring its people along. We ended up winning the contract because we suggested that the "HP Way" was better represented by embracing people in the change effort and using their judgment to gain commitment to those changes.

Six Sigma is another great example of a well-respected methodology for improving organizational performance. However, time and again we see that its success is linked directly to the levels of true ownership, commitment, and accountability, rather than to the number of meetings people attend or the levels of mere compliance with the process steps. In a market-leading multinational manufacturing organization we worked with, the CEO's engineering background and belief in the "science" of Six Sigma drove him to ensure his managers and employees were rigorously complying with the process rather than truly owning the need to improve quality and the customer experience. As a result, Six Sigma was pervasive but customer satisfaction and quality levels continued to decline. No customer ever proclaimed, "Wow, I love what they're doing with Six Sigma," or "Quality teams have really improved my loyalty!"

Thus this lesson: Organizational commitment to a CEO's strategy is a key factor, perhaps *the* key factor, in the success of the strategy and its organizational objectives. The degree to which employees will travel the last mile to execute that strategy makes the difference between stellar results and mediocrity, and sometimes any results at all.

Why, then, is this such a mystery for executives?

Most Leaders Confuse Compliance and Commitment

The type of *commitment* to which we have been referring is absent in most organizations—that's right, *most*. Compounding the crime is the fact that leadership usually doesn't realize it. For example, when revenue and/or profits are suffering, executives rarely focus on a deficiency in commitment as the source or the cause. Instead, they round up Claude Rains's "usual suspects": competitor action, poor sales initiatives, lack of management oversight, economic woes, and so forth. (You might like to know that we serve on a number of boards, and perhaps the most egregious example comes from nonprofit arts leadership. They will cite a bad economy for the arts whenever projections aren't met, never caring to discuss arts groups that *are* doing quite well.)

Consequently, many CEOs avoid dealing with commitment issues, no less than a man on his twenty-fifth date with a woman who is impatient to make some more permanent plans. The CEO assumes that commitment is never a problem, largely because the CEO assumes everyone is equally committed.

> **StratComment**
>
> *"Projection" is the psychological conveying of one's own strengths and weaknesses to others. That's never more dangerous than when executives believe that if they are committed, everyone must be as well.*

When executives work until eight o'clock at night, they sometimes expect others to follow their lead. We all know how well that works out. Those who may stay, due to guilt or aspirations or fear, seldom do so with high productivity. They feel *forced* into staying, but they are not *committed* to staying. (Perhaps the boss ought to be "committed" for believing otherwise.)

Executives tend to underestimate the impact of noncommitment and believe that if people are merely doing their jobs without interruption and abiding by the organization's rules and procedures, then all is well. But that false belief is the essence of mistaking compliance for commitment. It's the difference between the receptionist who packs up at 4:50 p.m. and waits for the clock to strike 5:00 before bolting out the door, and the one who hears the phone ring at 5:05 on her way out and goes back to answer it. It's the distinction between the salesperson who has reached her optimal bonus potential and is "loafing" until next year, and the one who keeps plugging away to set new records because it's well known that the company needs all the revenue it can muster this year. As one fellow said while introducing himself during a meeting we were attending, "I can't remember how long I've been here, but I have fifty-four months to go." Hard to imagine how many innovative ideas he contributed each week!

Another vivid example was offered by an employee (we'll call him Mike) at a rubber chemicals plant where we were brought in as consultants. His first day on the job was ten years earlier, and Mike was shown the ropes by a veteran. The job he was assigned to do— filling large burlap bags with a powdery white compound and then stacking them—looked fairly straightforward. Deciding he wanted to make a good impression on his workmates, Mike worked as hard as he could to beat the veteran's explicit declaration: "We do fifty bags per shift." Filling eighty-two bags on his first shift, Mike was pleased with himself and enthusiastically reported his accomplishment to his peers. Mike failed to understand the grumblings from the others; the next day he produced eighty-seven bags during his shift. The following day there was a scratch on Mike's car. By the end of his first week, Mike got the message and started consistently delivering his fifty bags per shift just like everyone else.

Most likely, those CEOs who are oblivious to such corporate dynamics haven't experienced the robust nature and extraordinary levels of performance that true commitment generates, because they haven't been amidst it before. The current reality may seem to be "as good as it gets," according to the mental set of someone who is racing to put out fires all the time, so that even a brief lull with mere embers represents an oasis in the day's journey. In some cases they have tried before to generate enthusiasm and energy and it didn't work for any number of reasons, so they have given up on dramatic improvement.

Their etiology is wrong, and their resultant actions are doomed.

Many leaders are simply out of touch with the sentiments of employees, which is the height of irony, since human resources departments often fill their time with a plethora of employee surveys and assessments (more about this in chapter 9). Blindfolded and in a soundproofed chamber, we can nevertheless report the results of two-thirds of those samplings: There's always poor communication and low morale, and employees say they feel disposable and there's no respect for opinions—do you get the picture? At which point HR brings in an external training firm to fix the problem, but unfortunately this action, too, focuses on the wrong thing.

More often than not, "morale problems" are avoided, delegated, or swept under the plants out in the parking lot because they are amorphous monsters that no one cares to deal with. ("I'm committed, and so is my team, so why aren't those ingrates?") Doesn't a morale problem, after all, reflect poorly on senior management? We really can't have that kind of thing here, management tells itself.

So self-images are preserved, new gurus are brought in, and the discussion continues about whether or not the employees we have are the right people. They *are* of course, the right people (in most cases), but they are not *committed* people. No matter how "right" the person is, he cannot act "right" if he isn't committed to the organizations values, direction, and goals.

Sometimes commitment issues are finally dealt with after the barn door is open, the horses have departed, the barn is in disrepair, and a horde of bats have taken over the place. We have seen direct reports plead the commitment case and be ignored: "You're going to have to be tougher and show more than just soft skills if you expect to head one of the subsidiaries." We once heard some reporters at the American Press Institute say that the whole commitment and motivation thing is ridiculous, especially in journalism. Throw people in a room, lock the doors, they claimed, and occasionally throw in some fresh meat. The strong will survive and perform.

As a rule, when performance and effectiveness begin to decline (quality of work, responsiveness, customer satisfaction, new sales, repeat business, and so on), the commitment factor isn't tracked or challenged. Yet we've all seen commitment plunge at companies such as US Airways, Dell, Maytag, and Ford. And we have also seen commitment be resurrected, as has happened at Apple, IBM, and Continental Airlines. (Interestingly, commitment never seems to vary from high ground at FedEx, GE, Levi Strauss, or Ritz-Carlton.) Once the indices decline, it is tougher and tougher to restore commitment.

Organizational reality does not have to be this way. Including and engaging employees so that they can fully commit to the strategy is *the* ultimate factor in whether strategy succeeds or not, because strategy *never fails in its formulation, only in its execution.*

Every CEO and leadership team has the potential to generate high levels of commitment. We have mentioned the examples above because they are cross-industrial, cross-hierarchical, and cross-cultural. We have seen Westerners scoff at Japanese businesses where employees and management commonly partake of exercise or meditation in the mornings before the start of the workday. Yet these are practices that help gain inclusion and commitment in their culture. It is not an "Asian belief system" that makes Toyota so strong, but the inclusion of its people in every aspect of quality, including the right to stop an entire assembly line when an imperfection is detected downstream (which, by the way, means the upstream people are very careful not to allow imperfections).

Contrast that to most Western manufacturing operations, where management typically has cardiac arrest if a mere employee deigns to stop the flow of work.

Against these odds, we have found that every top team can generate commitment, even without the morning exercises and meditation. But it takes quite a bit of courage, and therein lies the rub.

Generating Commitment Requires Great Courage

Generating commitment is possible for any leadership team willing to follow some simple rules. The first rule is the toughest: brutal honesty.

We're not talking about being brutally honest with others, but rather about being brutally honest with oneself. The top team must confront the need for commitment and the current lack thereof. Managers don't want to admit that they are leading a unit with less than total commitment, because emotionally laden words arise that threaten their self-image, issues such as loyalty, candor, trust, belief, values, and so forth. Yet only when leaders are willing to "own" the current state of affairs, and admit to themselves that they have *caused* the current levels of apathy, resistance, or resignation, can they begin to address and improve the situation.

That's because you cannot "fix" lack of commitment without addressing the cause, and the cause is almost always leadership's failure to appreciate the priority of commitment.

StratComment
The first step in gaining and/or improving commitment is for leaders to admit to their accountability for the current lack of commitment. If leadership doesn't look into the mirror, nothing will change about the image.

An inescapable aspect of this honesty is confronting internal politics, silos, trust, and internecine warfare. This is usually a grueling and onerous challenge, as it should be, since these dynamics have been built and calcified over long periods of time. (No organization develops silos naturally. It is learned behavior emanating from those establishing the silos.) People are hardened to workplace environments where pretending, protecting, and propitiation are all too common. "CYA"* is often the unwritten priority at the top of everyone's to-do list.

These are toxic workplace dynamics, and the only effective solution is to have the courage to wade in and throw out the bad influences. When the CEO and the top team actually undertake this reversal with courage and conviction, they send an undeniable message to the rest of the organization: This is the new way. Lou Gerstner took just this action when IBM was suffering through horrible morale problems and trust issues. So, too, did Richard Clark at Merck. Clark was an inside promotion after the board fired the former CEO, Ray Gilmartin, who had been brought in from the outside and couldn't live up to the legacy of Roy Vagelos, the CEO who brought Merck to glory days.

Thus, both insiders and outsiders can effect such courageous change. It is a matter of leadership volition.

Two leaders, each running $1-billion-plus organizations—one a manufacturing firm and one a services firm—provide great comparisons. We observed immediately that each executive had tremendous commitment challenges to deal with. There was a lack of trust and poor alignment among levels and functions throughout the organizations, undermining ambitious and necessary growth plans.

The CEO of the services firm, having risen as a star from the sales ranks, was characterized as an arrogant leader. Despite repeated attempts by senior people to apprise him of the high levels of politics, distrust, and lack of commitment rampant in the organization, he characterized the situation as "a bunch of employees whining and not doing their jobs." He introduced aggressive cost reduction and rigid quality improvement initiatives that elicited no passion among key people. (Think of Al Dunlap at Sunbeam.)

---

* "Cover your ass."

His initiatives fell flat, and he was unsuccessful in his growth plans for the firm.

The CEO of the manufacturing entity was also a tough guy, having turned around two other divisions within the company. When his management team criticized the levels of trust and collaboration across departments, he listened over several weeks without taking any action. Instead, he observed evidence of what they claimed. Ultimately he decided the commitment issue was serious enough to launch a process to improve it. This wasn't easy for someone accustomed to quick strikes and dramatic actions. But he understood the need and critical nature of commitment. His results were spectacular, both in terms of meeting corporate performance objectives as well as creating an unprecedented platform of cross-functional collaboration and partnership that was a model for the company.

Two CEOs, two commitment problems. One discounted and dismissed the issue; the other faced it, took accountability for it, and transformed it. Two very different outcomes resulted.

We don't use the term *courageous* loosely. Leaders must take the initiative to overcome the roadblocks that delay organizational movement.

We were asked to work with the CEO of a major, privately held, billion-dollar health organization. He reported to an owner, but had complete authority in the company. His COO was a much younger man, but he was with the organization longer and had been passed over for the top spot when the current CEO was recruited from another industry.

The sparks flew immediately. The younger man undermined the CEO on every occasion. Since the operating units reported to the COO, two huge combative forces of subordinates formed. However, this was no chess match—it was more like cage fighting. At one point the COO openly challenged the CEO at a company dinner attended by scores of senior people and their spouses, and the CEO heatedly responded, as everyone else stared at their soup.

Commitment was given to one of the two men by most managers, not to the organization or its mission. Now, listen carefully: When the CEO was asked how long this situation had been going on, he said, "Nine years."

Nine years!

The CEO thought he could patch the problem with a little time and money. When he realized it would take a much more significant investment to *transform* this issue, his response was classic for someone who refuses to assume a courageous position: "Oh, I could never invest that much time or money, and it would give the COO more fodder for his cannons."

Think of the lost productivity, lost talent, poorer patient/customer services, and wasted money lavished on this divisiveness, the antithesis of commitment.

We present these tales because we are sure you have seen similar, incredible waste and futility. These are not apocryphal stories. They occur every day in organizations where compliance trumps commitment and the organization is consumed by egos, turf protection, politics, and fear.

The greatest single factor in behavior change in organizations is the avatar—that person to whom others look for examples of action. It doesn't matter what kind of organization it is. Within any organization, people don't believe what they read or what they hear. They only believe what they *see*.

If they see leaders who create division and personal fiefdoms, who demand respect rather than earn it, and who don't understand the importance of commitment, they will emulate that behavior at their levels, and assume such behavior is best for promotion, tenure, and safety.

But if they see leaders who strive to *build* commitment, then they will do the same. It's that tough. It's that courageous. And it's that simple.

◆ ◆ ◆

CHAPTER 2

WHAT IS STRATEGIC COMMITMENT?

If It's So Important, Why Don't I Know About It?

Most corporate initiatives fail. That's right, you read it here: Most fail. The scorecard doesn't show a great many runs and is rife with errors.

Our experience, globally, is that cost cutting, revenue enhancement, improved customer satisfaction, even employee retention initiatives are not accomplished to the extent desired, within the time frame established, or within the budget allocated. In fact, Professor Robert Kaplan of the Harvard Business School and his associate, David Norton at the Balanced Scorecard Collaborative, have researched this issue and estimate that as much as *90 percent of all corporate strategies are not executed successfully.*

Other than that, they work very well.

There's Commitment and There's *Commitment*

We are all aware of the struggle Hewlett-Packard had in digesting its competitor Compaq, with the resultant earnings drop, loss of repute, and ultimate firing of CEO Carly Fiorina. Global titan FedEx had significant problems in many overseas markets. The subprime financial world was ignoring clear economic

indicators in 2007 or had faith in illusory controls and contin-
gencies.

There are many examples of poor planning and worse implementation. However, economists and consultants are fond of saying, "On
the other hand. . . ."

So consider this: In the telecommunications industry, the leaders
of Lucent's (then Avaya's) nascent U.S. indirect channels organization reached a revenue goal ten times higher than projected over just
three years—growing the business to $1.7 billion—after skeptical
managers stopped harping and criticizing and began supporting and
innovating in what executives referred to as "a culture of unstoppable
commitment."

Or consider this: Capital One's treasury function, a not atypically
perceived "staff function" and traffic cop within most organizations,
metamorphosed into a key supporter of the company's double-digit
growth in the face of capital market turbulence and regulatory hurdles.

Why do some organizations, albeit a minority, succeed in their
initiatives and strategies while most stumble like a drunkard walking
on cobblestones?

Because there is commitment and then there is *commitment.*

Everyone would readily agree that commitment is important, yet
most firms too readily accept compliance masquerading as commitment. As we stated in chapter 1, *compliance* is the acceptance of
alternatives by the workforce because there is no choice and there
are often penalties for noncompliance. *Commitment* is the vigorous,
voluntary support of initiatives by the workforce that they participate in formulating and/or implementing, and for which they take
complete ownership.

Motivation is intrinsic. You cannot "motivate" someone else.
However, outstanding managers can create environments conducive
to people motivating themselves. That is a huge distinction, and the
reason, by the way, that blanket "motivational programs" seldom
work. Nirvana for you is cough syrup for us.

What Drives True Commitment?

True commitment is a function of leaders focusing on both the *content* and *context* aspects of their strategy, which we'll discuss in the next section. But for now, let's make this clear: Our experience is unequivocal. Leaders such as Lou Gerstner at IBM, Herb Kelleher at Southwest Airlines, and Steve Jobs at Apple shift their workforce into a state of strategic commitment—*a condition of total ownership and alignment for the organization's direction and goals, and a self-imposed accountability for its success.*

Most "commitment" does not involve these elements to this degree. Hence, beyond "compliance" there is a "pseudo commitment" wherein employees feel aware of, and even interested in, the organization's direction and goals, yet they are not supportive. That's why there is "commitment" and then *commitment*—which we're calling Strategic Commitment. The latter state only occurs when employees are passionately sharing in the ownership and accountability for achieving new levels and standards.

One of the distinguishing characteristics of the three leaders above is that they created clear styles so that everyone viewed them in a certain manner. Gerstner, Kelleher, and Jobs* were visible, serving as exemplars, and quite vocal. And within their organizations, scores of senior managers adopted the same behaviors. These are the people we don't readily know and who are seldom recognized beyond the office, but who form the key cohort to set the example for ongoing, cascading commitment throughout the organization.

Here's another example: Lucent's real estate division (prior to the merger with Alcatel) cut costs *by more than $100 million* and had to gain unprecedented support from its major union to make the requisite workplace changes. The executive leading the turnaround—Tony

---

* At this writing, Steve Jobs has taken a temporary break from Apple's helm to attend to his health.

Marano—had been perceived by union leaders as highly effective, but harsh and controlling. He had to understand and change his style (perception *is* reality, after all, and informs the behavior of others) before the union would agree to participate in radical changes. That is the hallmark of outstanding appreciation of the need for true commitment.

Aside from the personal behavior adjustments required of leaders, there are process and structural adjustments that can be key to creating organization-wide commitment. Leaders often have to embrace a great many others within the strategy formulation process in order to make them feel included. This process can entail delays and even friction internally, but those are the tolls required to travel the road of commitment. Marano was able to learn new leadership behaviors and norms. He was the avatar for personal responsibility for change.

If he could do it, so could the union leaders and the employees.

Lee Iacocca was back with a new book in 2007, and his history as the Chrysler turnaround champion has been so thoroughly examined as to be old news. But Iacocca's behaviors remain the standard today: He put himself on the line as company spokesman. He "personally" guaranteed quality; took the heat from Congress in asking for funds; went to the union to ask for collaboration, not capitulation; and was the pointman for innovative new products, including the trend-setting minivan and the reintroduction of the convertible into American mainstream auto production.

Commitment starts with the leader, permeates through the senior ranks, and then "infects" everyone with a willingness and urgency to reach new heights through personal accountability and improvement.

The Heart of Strategic Commitment: Content and Context

There are two key dimensions to gaining and perpetuating strategic commitment: *content* (which most executives understand) and *context* (which is usually ignored).

Let's begin with content, which itself includes two drivers: *validity* and *clarity*.

Content: Validity

The typical approach to developing the content of a strategy often involves using an internal strategy group (consisting of ex-consultants who are tired of traveling week after week), cross-functional teams, and/or outside consultants. They will work for months and months to develop objectives and plans as they attempt to ensure the relevance and accuracy of the strategic approach: Can we be certain that this strategy, at this time, with these assumptions, is the right one for our organization?

Content: Clarity

In most cases, a major communications campaign happens next, to try to guarantee that the messages are clear. The public relations staff, corporate communications personnel, and others may be involved. There are meetings and memos; videotapes and feature stories in house organs are produced; hot lines and all kinds of mechanisms are established to try to ensure everyone understands the content of the strategy.

These two drivers, validity and clarity, may satisfy the executive team that strategy is well in hand, and that the key issue is now ensuring everyone in the organization understands it. However, that is seldom the reality. For one thing, a "thermal zone" exists in virtually all organizations that refracts messages, just as light is refracted at differing water levels and temperatures (see Figure 2-1).

For example, the head of strategy at the international division of a major financial services company spent months building a strategy to increase European market share, reiterating it, and socializing it throughout his organization. Although he had gathered and included input from his peers in preparing the

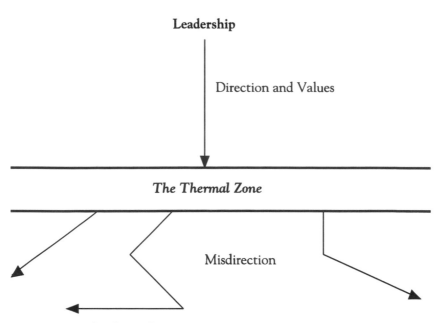

Figure 2-1. The thermal zone.

strategy, upon completion those same senior managers resisted what they believed to be *his* plan being imposed on *them*. What he failed to understand was that creating a feeling of true involvement and commitment requires much more than the socializing of content.

Even this seemingly straightforward idea of getting everyone on the same page about content is not effectively implemented in many organizations. So often when we talk to leaders about their key challenges, different executives have varying—and even contradictory—interpretations about the direction, the strategy, and the key objectives. Some say it's clear and it's right or left; others say it's not clear, or it's more left than right—and this is at the senior manager level! The lower in the organization you go, the worse it gets. We frequently hear leaders say, "We spent two days agreeing on our key imperatives for the year, only to see later on that everyone had gone back to work on their own things."

The Drivers of Context

Getting people behind the strategy doesn't begin and end with perfecting its content. The CEO must also focus on the *context* of the strategy—people's decisive beliefs that ultimately determine success or failure. These beliefs fall into four categories:

1. Whether leaders and managers are perceived as *credible* and *sincere*. Do people believe the leaders and managers will be straight with them about what is really going on?

2. Whether leaders and managers are perceived as having the *courage* and *resolve* to see the strategy through. Will they be open to hearing the real, often negative feedback, and will they have the guts to deal with the real issues? Will they stay the course in the face of adversity?

3. Whether the leaders are perceived as *competent* in creating and executing the strategy. Do people believe their leaders know what they are doing?

4. Whether people believe their leaders and managers truly *care* about the impact of the initiative on them. Will the leaders and managers ensure that people see the benefits, are able to contribute, and are recognized for that contribution? Will management care about them as human beings, or will they view them as mere instruments to achieve their goals?

Let's further explore each context driver.

Context: Credibility and Sincerity

The only thing harder than gaining trust is losing it and trying to regain it. If employees don't believe their leaders are sincere, they will have serious doubts and fears about the new direction, particularly if it calls for layoffs and cost reductions. They will also question just about everything else said about the strategy, including the very need for it. They will continuously feel leaders are in it for themselves, and they'll wonder, "What's the hidden agenda? What is not being said? What's really going to happen?"

At Lucent's real estate division, Marano promised the executive committee significantly lower costs and increased efficiency—results that would not be achieved easily. Two-thirds of the division's 2,500 employees were unionized, and union/management relations were contentious. Marano told union management and employees that they had to improve productivity and reduce costs, although he didn't ask for job reductions. However, the union distrusted Marano and other managers, believing that once they finished streamlining processes they would lay off union workers or hand their work over to nonunion labor.

The union had reasons to doubt Marano's sincerity. Management made many prior decisions unilaterally—decisions benefiting the company at the expense of union workers. Perceiving Marano to be insincere, union leaders refused to cooperate in meetings for planning the changes in the workplace. Within the limits of their contract, union members slowed down their work, handicapping the initiative. Only after directly addressing the union's concerns and demonstrating their sincere intent to build collaboration were Marano and his managers able to elicit commitment and involvement from the union members. This effort allowed for levels of partnership, teamwork, and productivity that were considered exemplary within the industry.

> **StratComment**
>
> *Commitment is just like trust; the only thing worse than no trust is having had it and lost it.*

Context: Courage and Resolve

Everyone may understand a strategy. However, they won't get fully on board if they believe their leaders and managers lack the courage and resolve to follow through. When employees doubt the openness and courage of their leaders and managers to deal with the real and tough issues facing the organization and to stay the course, including hearing bad news about the business or about themselves, they will silently resort to going through the motions rather than lean in and help overcome inertia.

Worries about courage play out differently at varying levels of a company. At the senior level, the leadership team may worry that the CEO will not be open to entertaining tough conversations or making difficult decisions in key areas such as *strategy* (e.g., killing off unprofitable products or business units), *personnel* (e.g., removing incompetent, unproductive, or uncooperative executives or managers), *resources* (e.g., making necessary investments in technology or training and development), or *corporate politics* (e.g., challenging the entrenched bureaucracy).

Despite the CEO's pronouncements on the critical need for change, middle managers are likely to fear that senior leaders will not "walk the talk." They worry that their bosses will opt out and not be admonished for it because of internal politics and a culture that doesn't hold people accountable. That makes it unsafe for employees to raise difficult issues—the real stuff that challenges the politics, norms, and organizational status quo.

In addition, failed change programs of the past will dent people's beliefs about the resolve of their leaders and managers *this time*. Despite leaders' repeated declarations about their commitment to this change effort, people will remain skeptical. The mugs, pens, posters, and other motivational accoutrements that the organization has purchased will be seen as a sure sign that this too shall pass.

When Capital One, the fast growing financial institution heavily reliant on reputation-sensitive capital markets for funding, disclosed that its federal banking regulators had concerns about the company's controls and governance, the firm's treasury department acutely felt increased pressures in funding the company. Rating agencies and investors reacted negatively to the disclosure, making it more challenging to secure the funding necessary to keep the company's credit card business growing at a double-digit rate. "People around the company thought we were exaggerating the challenges we faced in the markets and were becoming obstacles," recalls Steve Linehan, executive vice president and head of treasury. "I guess I could understand their view because we had always found a way to fuel our enormous growth in the past despite our below-investment grade ratings and relatively short track record. The reality was this had become a different ball game." The criticism only heightened the frustration of his associates, who were working 70-80 hour weeks with, in their minds, little appreciation of their efforts in the face of significant challenges.

To get his associates behind the initiative to improve their situation, Linehan first had to demonstrate his commitment to their wellbeing and his resolve in correcting inequities in workload, cumbersome processes and incentives. In an environment full of corporate initiatives to contain costs, Linehan took his headcount issues directly to Capital One's CEO Rich Fairbank. "Rich recognized that a relatively small increase in headcount would be of tremendous help in putting billions of dollars of great business on the books," says Linehan. Even though addressing some of the headcount and process issues would take the better part of a year to complete, Linehan's people were more willing to get behind his improvement initiative because he had the courage to address contentious issues and the resolve to get the resources necessary to alleviate the workload problem.

Context: Competency

The most powerful leadership is not hierarchical, where power is bestowed by dint of title. Nor is it the ability to reward and punish, because these measures can often be circumvented and a big stick isn't effective unless it is constantly present. And it's not sheer expertise, because a content expert isn't necessarily the best person to lead others forward.

Leaders' competence will be assessed based on the ways they exercise judgment on critical issues, and on their perceived ability to deliver on the promises they make, and to inspire others to follow them. People will be quite reticent to follow when they feel their leader is in over his or her head, or making commitments that are too big a stretch from previously demonstrated skills, knowledge and abilities. Managers will quickly shy away from aligning themselves with objectives they feel their bosses are making that are beyond the bounds of achievability.

The most effective leadership is *referent*, meaning that other people truly believe they should follow the leader because the leader is competent to help them and protect them. The best of such leaders are called *charismatic*. A lack of perceived competence held back the executive team at MSL's Arden Hills' facility from working together to improve their flagging performance. The manufacturing and engineering functions were frustrated with each other, the result of long disputes over who was at fault for chronic customer dissatisfaction. Engineering did not feel that manufacturing was competent; they did not believe that instructions were followed rigorously or that sufficient care was taken to meet client expectations. Manufacturing did not feel that Engineering understood the challenges they faced in manufacturing product. They blamed Engineering for incomplete and insufficient communication to enable them to successfully manufacture products. When customers complained about quality or shipping delays, each group pointed fingers at each other, often times resulting in the loss—or certainly the dismay—of that customer. "With each side doubting the other's competence, we had a dark outlook on our future," says Margit Elo, VP and General Manager. In chapter 3 we'll complete this example by showing how they addressed these issues, helping them become the most profitable plant in MSL's portfolio.

Context: Care and Concern

Everyone may believe these three conditions—leaders' sincerity, competence, and courage—are present in their company, business unit, or division. However, they must also believe that they will personally benefit from supporting the strategy—financially, developmentally, in their ability to contribute and be recognized, or perhaps in other, more personal ways. People must also feel that their management cares about them on a human level in order to commit fully to the initiative. Typically, we find leaders and managers who assume that what's compelling to them—improvements in revenue, cost, time-to-market, shareholder returns, and other aspects of organizational performance—will also be motivating to employees. If only it worked that way. In fact, very often employees at all levels of the organization—including executive team members themselves—do not feel the connection between organizational gain and their personal investment and benefits. They may, in fact, believe the new initiative will be to their disadvantage.

Concerns about the personal impact of a change initiative play out somewhat differently at each organizational level. Senior executives wonder whether the initiative will increase their opportunities in the organization. Those who see fewer opportunities (especially in relation to others) will withhold or temper their commitment. Middle managers will often feel their input is not being sought. They are closer to the day-to-day challenges of implementing the changes, yet they feel burdened with the egos and turf issues of leaders who they believe do not understand the difficulty in making those changes.

Money is not the ultimate motivator, though its absence is certainly a demotivator. In other words, if you give an unhappy employee more money, you have a *wealthier* unhappy employee. People need to feel cared for. They need and want to feel their leaders have their interests in mind, *even if* the condition and direction of the organization mean some individuals will ultimately need to find employment elsewhere. In situations where people leave organizations on good terms, feeling appropriately cared for, they remain positive customers and advocates of the company far more often than when they are treated as Mark Langford of The Accident Group infamously treated his employees—texting them a message not to show up for work the next day. (Langford's U.K. firm—which promulgated the idea that "where there's blame, there's a claims compensation case"—went bust and notoriously fired its 2,500 staff with a text message that read: "Urgent. Unfortunately salaries not paid. Please do not contact office. Full details to follow later today." They and many of the firm's clients were left without a penny.)

Nevertheless, the more that people believe that management values them as resources and not as expenses, the more committed they tend to become. When Gordon Bethune was CEO of Continental Airlines, he was faced with the daunting challenge of moving the company from last to first as a preferred business travelers' airline. In the process, he established key performance areas (e.g., baggage delivery, on-time arrivals) and guaranteed bonuses if the airline finished in the top one or two spots in each area.

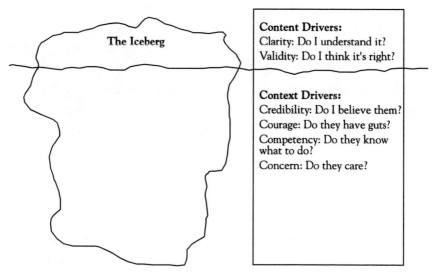

The Iceberg

Content Drivers:
Clarity: Do I understand it?
Validity: Do I think it's right?

Context Drivers:
Credibility: Do I believe them?
Courage: Do they have guts?
Competency: Do they know what to do?
Concern: Do they care?

Figure 2-2. The "iceberg" of strategy.

And that's exactly what happened. (One year they finished third, but Bethune called it an example of poorly compiled statistics and paid the bonus anyway.) Those who see personal opportunity and appreciation for their contribution will provide tremendous commitment.

As Figure 2-2 illustrates, more obvious elements of strategy—the content—are readily visible. But the underlying elements—the context—are beneath the surface, yet are the key drivers of strategic commitment.

The Characteristics of a Strategic Commitment Environment: Why Should You Care That They Don't Care?

Organizations whose strategy is valid and clear (high on content) but whose employees don't trust their leaders' credibility, courage, competence, and care (low on context) will at best produce an environment of uninspired compliance. While employees may well understand the plan and believe it is right, they won't believe their leaders will be able to implement the plan (or implement it without harmful effects). Hence, they will resort to "going along" with little sense of ownership, enthusiasm, and commitment. In the absence of ownership and accountability, the leaders will resort to managing through dictate, mandate, and command and control. This will undermine people's desire to go the next level of performance and produce exceptional results. This may be efficient, but ultimately ineffective.

Conversely, if context is high and content is low (see Figure 2-3), employees will be highly motivated to make a weak strategy work. Eventually, however, their excitement won't be enough to overcome the bad plan and weak structure. The result will be failure coupled with cynicism and resignation.

Of course, when both content and context are low, employee morale will hit rock bottom. Believing in neither the plan nor the leaders behind it, employees will be hugely cynical and often oppositional.

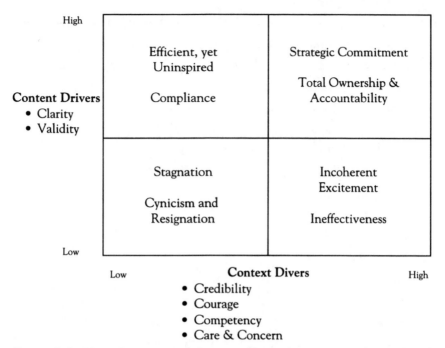

Figure 2-3. How Content and Context Shape Organizational Mood and Effectiveness.

But when content and context are both high, everyone will believe in the plan—and in the leaders' ability to make it happen in ways that aren't injurious to people's careers. This will produce a state of strategic commitment, one in which everyone understands and believes in the strategy and feels total ownership and accountability to make it happen.

Leaders can turn apathy into strategic commitment—if they know how to detect, address, and transform content and context issues quickly and effectively.

StratComment

Strategic Commitment reflects the marriage of Strategy and Commitment. Strategy without Commitment is theory; Commitment without Strategy is hype.

While on an assignment for Aon Insurance, we visited a claims office in Syracuse to evaluate its daily performance. Leaving a meeting at about 5:10 p.m., we noticed a receptionist packing her things to leave when the phone rang. Without hesitation, she sat down with her coat on and answered the phone.

When she was done with the call she recognized us and said, "Good night." We asked her how things were going. "Just great," she said, "our claims ratio is exceeding our goals."

Stunned, we asked, "What do you mean?"

"Well, a claims ratio is a measure of premium income versus claims paid . . . ," she began. "We know that," we said, "but why is it important to you?"

"Every Friday our manager gets all of us together and explains the impact we're all having on local, regional, and corporate goals, and asks for suggestions on how we can improve. The claims ratio is one of those goals," she explained.

What had happened here?

Management shared goals with employees, ensuring the goals were clear and well understood. And they demonstrated they cared about their employees by asking them for ideas to meet and beat the goals, and involving them in weekly progress reports (among a host of other things).

In other words, in an apathetic environment, that receptionist is packed up and ready to leave at 4:50 p.m. and won't answer the phone after that time because a complicated request or urgent problem might keep her past five. But a committed employee is in no big rush to leave and sees it as the most natural act in the world to answer a ringing phone no matter what the time.

Organizations can certainly advance and gain success with apathetic employees, or at least apathetic employees who are moved to strict compliance. The pyramids were built without commitment on the part of the workforce, but rather with the constant application of coercion: flogging and death. The old bromide, "The beatings will cease as soon as morale improves," is not the product of a science fiction writer but more the accurate reporting of a documentary filmmaker.

You should care about an apathetic workforce because it costs you money every day, creates far more layers of management than are really required, and can advertently or inadvertently sabotage your strategic goals. Even the slaves building the pyramids of Egypt attempted to slow down progress, feigned excuses and injuries, ignored defects in the construction, and constantly planned to escape. As Frederick Taylor so eloquently wrote in his 1911 book *The Principles of Scientific Management*:

> So universal is soldiering for this purpose [of keeping managers ignorant of how fast work can be done] that hardly a competent workman can be found ... who does not devote a considerable part of his time to studying just how slow he can work and still convince his employer that he is going at a good pace. Under our system a worker is told just what he is to do and how he is to do it. Any improvement he makes upon the orders given to him is fatal to his success.

Have you considered the expenditures you are currently enduring, if not actually encouraging, in employees who:

- Require layers of supervision and the concomitant expense
- Find excuses to arrive late, leave early, and minimize contribution
- Spend time on personal issues, second jobs, and recreation while at work
- Undermine the efforts of colleagues through their urging or their examples of neglecting work
- Alienate customers by providing inadequate service and responsiveness
- Fail to point out errors, omissions, and problems that will cause expense and embarrassment later

◻ Never offer a new idea or innovation to improve the business, which, competitively, needs new ideas every day

We could go on, but you get the idea. The more your frontline employees are active in transmitting experiences and ideas and implementing new approaches, the more you are able to innovate. The more you must problem-solve and "fix" things, the more your workforce has let you down by not identifying weaknesses early or by ignoring them. We have long observed that organizations with massive quality efforts and Six Sigma approaches needed these interventions *precisely because employees were not naturally engaged in problem prevention and identification*—that is, context issues were not being addressed. That's right: Massive quality programs are often an indication of a previously apathetic workforce that is going to become compliant only through strict measures and evaluation (coercion) and an assortment of contests and rewards (normative pressure).

But they still may not be very committed, meaning the quality program still hasn't solved the most basic quality problem of all—context issues.

In 1990, Cadillac Motor Car Company won the prestigious Malcolm Baldrige National Quality Award for most improved organization in terms of quality and defects removed. But the issue most people missed was that Cadillac was so terrible in the years before that it was far easier for it to show progress. The real question is: Were those employees who were so apathetic before still apathetic and simply working with a temporarily harsher light on them?

When Ford Motor Company acquired Jaguar, also back in 1990—and at the time, Ford was hardly a bastion of tremendous quality and commitment—the Ford engineers visiting a Jaguar manufacturing plant were astonished to find an entire team of workers located at the end of the assembly line and assigned specifically to fix the inevitable defects that the "completed" car would still have. Meanwhile, Toyota had embraced its workforce and empowered each person to stop the line to fix any defect, no matter how minor.

Apathetic employees kill a business. It can be a lingering and slow death, such as Jaguar, which has since been sold again, still endures. (Hopefully for Jaguar, its new owners at Tata Industries will be able to help right this condition.) Or it can be a quick exit, such as Langford's Accident Group.

You Might as Well Find Out Where You Stand Before Reading On

Perhaps you are thinking that you are in the advanced ranks of strategic commitment, and maybe you are. Or you may be receiving mixed signals about your leadership team's ability to create strategic commitment.

Fair enough. This is as good a time as any to determine where you stand. If you are still uncertain as to whether strategic commitment makes sense, then there's not much more we can do to convince you. But our experience indicates that most of you constitute the choir to whom we've been preaching, so the questions become:

1. Where do we stand, and is there room for improvement?
2. How do we sustain and nurture our strategic commitment once we've got it?
3. With whom do these accountabilities reside?

The Strategic Commitment Scorecard, which you'll find in the Appendix, will tell you exactly where you are starting this journey.

Are you willing to commit? There is no compliance for leaders. They need to commit or get out of the way.

CHAPTER 3

◆ ◆ ◆

WORKING BACK FROM THE FUTURE

How to Generate Strategic Commitment

Once a CEO is clear about the need for strategic commitment and embraces the premise that compliance pales compared to genuine commitment, which can only be achieved by addressing content and context issues, the key to success is "how." The important milestones for a leadership team on this journey are as follows (see also Figure 3-1):

1. Evaluate the current state of the organization to assess and improve leaders' ownership for the changes required.

2. Build a candid, cohesive, trusting team environment that recognizes and treasures mutual competence (instead of competition), and an environment in which truth is prized beyond deals and backroom agreements. This step addresses all context issues, expanding the team's capacity to develop and implement a strategy.

3. Create and align the leadership team behind a compelling and challenging strategy (the future state). This is the powerful *content* for the strategic execution.

4. Once the leadership team is unequivocally united behind the content and context, reach down into the rest of the organization to create alignment and engagement.

5. Reach out next to all key stakeholders, including customers,

to create a unity that is seamless, crosses departmental
boundaries, and aligns priorities.

6. Take action to ensure that the new content and context
   become the norm and are *sustainable*, building unstoppable
   momentum toward the intended strategic goals.

We're Not Here to Stick Our Toes in the Water, We're Here to Make Waves

Taking stock of the current reality means that the leadership team is
the key to igniting the process. The CEO must convince and enroll
subordinates in the need for a new direction vis-à-vis the current and
projected business conditions and the CEO's desire for something
beyond merely extrapolating yesterday's performance.

It won't surprise any readers to learn that we have found senior
teams not only to be on different pages, but sometimes reading different books! They tend to view the world from their silos, or foxholes,
or aeries. It doesn't matter; the view is seldom the same. Yet they
forge ahead, oblivious to the parallel tracks of their peers. (Santayana
remarked once that a fanatic is someone who loses sight of his objectives and consequently redoubles his efforts.) This creates a massive
lack of alignment and wastes resources, which are often deployed in
opposition to other areas, in blissful strategic ignorance.

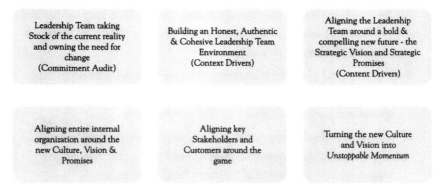

Figure 3-1. Key phases of the strategic commitment journey.

For example, a major IT reengineering project at Capital One was in its sixth month with little progress when Rob Alexander, the chief of strategy of their largest business, took it over.

Despite having a well-established project management office, Alexander found no one had an answer for the simple question: What are the specific objectives of this project and how far along are we in achieving them? The result: diffused energy, an inability to measure progress, and wasted time talking about a plan that didn't exist.

Although it took several weeks for Alexander and his team to clearly answer the question, once they did, the effectiveness of everyone on the project increased dramatically. By establishing better metrics, they were also able to measure their progress, which quickly accelerated. In addition, the leadership team's clarity and alignment enabled it to make significant changes in project direction—*including replacing the primary vendor*—while increasing momentum and morale. This clarity of focus and strong platform of alignment and partnership helped the group complete the three-year project on time and within budget, a feat highly uncommon in the world of mega-IT projects. (We provide a more complete description of this success story at the beginning of chapter 6.)

In our work with one of the divisions within a leading global telecommunications company—a team that is responsible for operationalizing global sales incentive programs worldwide—it became clear that there was a significant disconnect between the sentiments and perceptions of the regional field sales teams (their customers) about the effectiveness of their programs, and their effectiveness as a team in implementing them, and the perceptions and level of awareness within the operations team itself about these sentiments.

While the customers felt frustrated that the operations team was not listening, caring, and making the programs relevant and easy to implement, the operations leaders felt the only problem was that the regional field sales teams were being protective of their regions, noncollaborative, and not open to change (i.e., closed-minded). The operations leaders had little to no sense of the feelings of the field sales teams.

This dynamic had been going on for many months and frustrations were increasing. It was only when team members began to be honest about the current reality, which led to higher mutual awareness and ownership about this dysfunctionality, that the groups began to solve the issues and create better ways to work together. We see these dynamics in many companies. It is more the norm than the exception.

Honesty leads to candid awareness, which enables true ownership of the im-

> **StratComment**
> *The default position is usually one of singular, insulated, noncollaborative determination, which is antithetical to the context required for success.*

pediments to realizing a desired future state. Only then can you have a breakthrough in thinking and commitment, allowing for new possibilities, choices, behaviors, and outcomes. There are four elements to this sequence:

1. Leaders need to be willing and able to tell the truth about the current level of commitment in their organization in order to generate change. This process (described in chapter 1) requires courage; it means abandoning ego, admitting to uncertainties, and accepting challenge and ideas.

2. Only by being honest can leaders generate a sufficient level of awareness among themselves and throughout the organization about the content and context issues that need to be addressed; as a result, they will be able to own the current condition.

3. Ownership of the current condition—the good, the bad, and the ugly—is the prerequisite for generating breakthroughs (i.e., new possibilities and ways of doing things that have never been thought or done before). New possibilities always lead to new choices, actions, behaviors, and outcomes. Only owners feel the responsibility and accept the accountability to suggest and create change.

4. CEOs and their teams must tackle content and context issues head-on, because if they avoid and deny these issues (as they often do, unfortunately), it leaves them blind and out of touch with what is going on. When that happens, instead of owning the current condition, they start blaming others and circumstances for their plight. They avoid taking responsibility. When they fall off track (see Figure 3-2), they end up perpetuating the status quo and more of the same.

Barriers to Assessing the Current Reality

As covered in chapter 2, context issues are much more influential in terms of shaping actions and behaviors than those of content. And it's much harder for CEOs to face the truth about context issues than content, even though they are as blind to those issues, too.

So why do leaders ignore content and context issues?

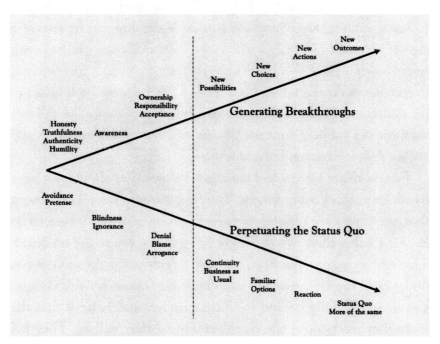

Figure 3-2. Two paths: generating breakthroughs versus perpetuating the status quo.

First, they are simply blind to them. While content issues are visible, context issues are invisible. Most executives believe that because they repeatedly present organizational imperatives at the equivalent of town hall meetings, everyone in the company therefore understands where they are headed and how to get there. But that only addresses the content dimension. Given that context issues are much more nuanced, executives are often clueless about weaknesses in that arena.

Second, managers have been taught for years that certain characteristics like supreme confidence, strategic thinking, decisiveness, and polished communications are desirable leadership attributes, so they focus on these things. In fact, these attributes and others often perpetuate context issues and erode commitment. (There'll be more about that in chapter 5.)

Third, dealing with context issues can be extremely uncomfortable for leaders because they threaten ego and status. And attending to matters of employee attitudes toward leadership can be seen as a sign of weakness. The CEO who lacks self-confidence will not want to put issues about his or his team's credibility, courage, competence, or intentions on the table. Even if the CEO believes he is aware of his shortcomings and how others view him and his team, he will fear that dealing publicly with such issues will expose his weakness and reduce people's confidence and respect.

Fourth, many leaders and managers believe they should not have to ask for people's commitment. They come from a school of thought that employees are obliged to execute an order when a boss issues it. It is a belief that "We shouldn't have to beg you to get on board. That's what we pay you for. This isn't a democracy. As soon as you understand the rationale and valid business reasons for this change, you should be fully behind it." These leaders also believe that the more they pay people, the more committed they will be. They fail to understand the difference between behaviors based on compliance and those based on a genuine desire to achieve something of significance. Money has never been the primary motivator in organizational settings, especially in terms of strategic adherence.

Fifth, providing incentives is only one part of the equation. If people do not feel their leaders are sincere, courageous, competent, and caring, they will default to compliance and pretense no matter how much they are paid. They will emulate their perception of their exemplars.

Sixth, executives don't pay attention to context and content issues because they don't recognize them as leading indicators of future performance. They think that as long as the results are there, everything is fine. In fact, the best *leading* indicators of the success of a strategy is the current strength of their content and context drivers, as these drivers directly shape the levels of alignment, ownership, and engagement among the people who need to implement the strategy.

What Are the Warning Signs?

To get executives to buy into the need for fundamental change, an unbiased and unvarnished assessment of their individual and collective views of the current content and context issues must be made. This "commitment audit" must examine the content and context issues at each level of the organization: the leadership team, the managerial ranks, and the entire employee population.

Our belief is that CEO Lou Gerstner instinctively did just such a commitment audit when he arrived at IBM, and that CEO Ray Gilmartin was blind to the need on entering Merck.

Quantitative instruments can help establish a baseline to measure the company's future progress in these areas, but even without them the leaders can still gauge the existing reality, if they really want to.

The commitment audit gives the leadership team invaluable insights into the most significant content and context issues. The most effective way to assess if and where there are commitment deficiencies is to observe people's behaviors. Here are some quite observable indicators:

- People do not speak up, even when they know things aren't being dealt with honestly and directly. This behavior is relatively easy to spot, especially in meetings. Everyone knows important issues are not being addressed. Yet they fail to speak up because of fear, apathy, or cynicism. We often ask people at all levels of the organization the simple question: "When and how many times have you been in a meeting where you know that something is not being said, and you know that others know it too, yet no one says anything?" People almost always admit this is a common occurrence. People speak up at FedEx, but not at UPS. They yell at Southwest Airlines, but don't make a peep at US Airways. They honk at Honda, but not at Ford.

- Missed commitments are met with excuses, explanations, rationalizations, and finger-pointing rather than a rigorous and enthusiastic desire to get to the source of the problem, get back on track, and take ownership for what went wrong. There are exceptions: Right after its runway debacles during the snowstorms of February 2007, JetBlue Airways accepted responsibility at the top and created a passengers' list of rights (which, ironically, a New York court struck down because it was deemed in conflict with federal laws).

- Problems are discussed and debated endlessly, with little lasting improvement from repeated attempts at resolution. We have all served on nonprofit boards where the same issues have been debated *for over a decade*. Many for-profit organizations are no different.

◻ Initiatives to improve organizational performance progress slowly or stall altogether, despite sizable investments in resources and technology. (See chapter 2, where we describe the organizational "thermal zone" that tends to redirect messages and hamper understanding of the company's direction and values.)

"Hallway" or watercooler conversations are also a good indicator. (We often refer to these as *background conversations*, because people may not hold these conversations in the open, due to fear, apathy, resignation, or numerous other logical but paralyzing reasons.) For example, when people spend time privately talking about how things are not their fault or how another department or organizational level is to blame for suboptimal results, commitment is lacking. When people privately complain about how busy they are rather than doing what needs to be done, this too can be a good indicator that people are avoiding rather than taking responsibility. Another sure sign: when employees complain about the unreasonableness of leaders' expectations. "I didn't meet my goals because the goals were wrong" is a chronic complaint indicative of this problem.

StratComment

Goals are sometimes wrong, but when they are called "wrong" after they are unmet, that is a sure sign of weak commitment. If they are in a trusting environment, committed people will speak up as soon as they see unreasonable goals, even when it's uncomfortable—they exercise courage.

Engaging people in a conversation aimed at exploring the real issues driving their behaviors is always very healthy. It is an informal way of discerning commitment problems. We suggest that CEOs who feel they may have such issues go beyond sensing to asking employees directly, engaging the members of their executive team and workers up and down the organization. In diagnosing the state of commitment in dozens of organizations, we have found questions such as these to be revealing.

Content-Related Questions

- To what degree do employees:

    1. Have a shared understanding and belief in the direction and objectives of the organization?

    2. Have a shared understanding and belief in the role of their function in meeting the objectives of the organization?

    3. Understand and believe in their personal role in helping to meet the objectives of the organization?

    4. Have a shared understanding and belief in how organizational success is measured?

Context-Related Questions

- To what degree do employees:

    1. Effectively address and resolve difficult issues?

    2. Take ownership for solving problems rather than make excuses or point fingers when things go wrong?

    3. Take risks and challenge the status quo?

    4. Have confidence in the leaders of the organization?

    5. Feel they can be honest with their leaders about negative or contentious issues—including about the leaders themselves?

    6. Feel connected with, and empowered by, their leaders?

    7. Communicate honestly and directly, without fear of retribution?

    8. Trust each other and work together effectively across departments?

9. Come to work every day feeling that they make a critical difference to the future of the business?

10. Feel enthusiastic about their work experience?

11. Feel appreciated for the work they do?

There are also proven assessment tools and surveys available to help gauge commitment and engagement. The Gallup Q12 is a particularly noteworthy survey tool where a 0.2 improvement along a five-point scale has been statistically proven to correlate with an increase in employee productivity.

A word of caution, however: If trust is low and fear is present, employees will not be truthful about the poor state of commitment. They must feel safe to tell it like it is. They must believe executives are genuinely interested in their unvarnished views, and they must feel encouraged to speak up about the real state of things, and praised when they do. Otherwise they will pay lip service to the process and say only the things they believe are safe. Unfortunately, this kind of lip service is more the norm than the exception.

Another question we often ask at all levels of organizations is: "How many of you come to work with the genuine experience that you make *the* difference in terms of the overall direction, spirit, and effectiveness of your organization?" While most people feel they make *a* difference within their own function or work environment, most also say they have limited impact on a larger scale. In fact, most people express views that other areas, functions, levels, or individuals have more influence on bigger issues. People talk in terms of the ubiquitous "them," as in "they" seem to be in control. While one could make a case about the validity (or lack thereof) of people's true ability to make *the* difference, we are alarmed by how pervasive these feelings of powerlessness are.

Figure 3-3 is a matrix that outlines the typical conversations employees at all organizational levels engage in when resistance, apathy, or compliance are displacing commitment.

Figure 3-3. *Hallway Conversations and Corresponding Behaviors.*

Content and Context Drivers	Impact on Conversations and Behavior	Impact at Different Organizational Levels		
		Executive Team	Middle Managers	Employees
		Content-Related		
When *Clarity* is in question	Flavor of "hallway" conversations	"We're not aligned on where we're headed."	"They can't even agree on where we're headed."	"The guys upstairs have no idea where we're going."
	Sentiments and behaviors	Conflicting agendas and recurring conflicts	Juggling multiple conflicting requests from above; confusion, irritation	Conflicting priorities, fire drills, frequent changes, frustration
When *Validity* is in question	Flavor of "hallway" conversations	"Why are we pursuing this direction? Is this really the right strategy?"	"This doesn't make sense. They never ask for our input."	"They don't understand what's going on around here—they are really disconnected."
	Sentiments and behaviors	Lip service, constantly revisiting decisions, tension and uncertainty	Hesitant compliance, minimal conviction, growing resentment	Grudging compliance, "do what you're told" attitude, increasing apathy and cynicism
		Context-Related		
When *Credibility* and *Sincerity* are in question	Flavor of "hallway" conversations	"We're not honest with each other—nobody puts all their cards on the table."	"I don't trust these guys. They always have a hidden agenda."	"They never tell us what's really going on—and we're the ones who will suffer, not them."
	Sentiments and behaviors	Caution, cover your ass (CYA), avoid tough issues, point fingers when things go wrong	Guarded compliance, continually looking for the hidden message	Going through the motions, cynicism, and distrust

When Courage is in question	Flavor of "hallway" conversations	"I'm not going to be the first to fall on my sword or make waves." "I won't call them on their stuff if they don't call me on mine."	"These guys don't have the guts to be straight about the real issues. All they care about is their own empire."	"It's dangerous to tell the truth around here because you'll get in trouble. Just lay low and don't rock the boat."
	Sentiments and behaviors	Paralysis by analysis, half-hearted commitments, silos, politics, risk aversion	Cover your ass, positioning, gamesmanship, frustration and cynicism	Cover your ass if something goes wrong, fear and cynicism
When Competency is in question	Flavor of "hallway" conversations	"These aren't people I'd choose to run this firm. I'm stuck with them, so I will make the best of things and look out for myself."	"They have no idea what it takes to get this done. They only care about status and position."	"If these guys knew what they were doing, we wouldn't be in this mess. They're getting big bucks and we're getting screwed."
	Sentiments and behaviors	Taking care of silos and people, turf protection, distrust of other silos	Going through the motions, resignation and frustration	Doing only as much as is absolutely required, cynicism
When Care and Concern are in question	Flavor of "hallway" conversations	"I'm only going to invest myself if I get favored or promoted."	"Here we go again: My input is not being sought, our contributions are going unnoticed. Nothing will change anyhow."	"What's the point? They will benefit and our lives will get harder and more stressful."
	Sentiments and behaviors	Self-promotion and turf protection, politics and positioning, defensiveness and anxiety	Uncertainty and fear, trying to figure out "What's in it for me?"	Avoiding rocking the boat so as not to be noticed, fear and self-preservation

These conversations and observable behaviors, when taken collectively, are powerful ways to assess the levels of credibility, courage, competence, care, and concern within the organization. The answers to these questions will provide deep insight into the context in which the strategy is being pursued and will let the CEO understand how much work needs to be done before embarking on a new strategic direction.

Diogenes Searching for the Honest Man

Before initiating any conversation about the content of a strategy (i.e., "where to go and how to get there"), it is critical the leadership team has a truly honest, authentic, courageous, and cohesive team environment in place in which people can really say what is on their minds and real decisions can be made with genuine alignment.

So often leadership teams discuss their strategic objectives and priorities in an environment that lacks those characteristics. Every time that happens you end up with situations in which everybody says "yes" to a direction in the public forum and then goes off and does their own thing, regardless. It is a frequent complaint we hear from executives who, nonetheless, seem befuddled by the phenomenon.

This situation only fuels more context issues within the leadership team and throughout the organization; the levels of trust and alignment within the leadership team are always replicated further down the organization.

Leaders always have opinions and sentiments about each other and the condition of the organization. Some are negative and some are positive. When the negative ones are not addressed they produce mischief. When the positive ones are not shared, they rob the team of the opportunity of reaching full potential.

Let's talk about negative opinions and sentiments, because they are more challenging for leaders to deal with. It is quite common, in fact, to find unhealthy dynamics between leadership team members. Executives often have negative assessments and sentiments about their peers' honesty, courage, competence, and concern for each other. When these sentiments go unexpressed, they fuel doubt, suspicion, distrust, and counterproductive interactions. (Usually the more negative the sentiments are, the less inclined leaders will be to address them, or they result in a "team building" effort that merely makes people temporarily feel better by tackling superficial topics.) These closely held but unspoken sentiments shape people's relationships to each other and to the future. As long as these stay unspoken—in the background—they continue to have a life of their own and produce mischief. "Perception is reality" is a function of the hallway or watercooler conversations that stay uncommunicated.

> **StratComment**
>
> *Leaders must encourage sharing both good news and bad news, positive feedback and negative feedback. It is as dangerous not to exploit the positive as it is to ignore the negative.*

To build an authentic, honest, courageous environment, the leadership team needs to be willing and able to put these hallway conversations on the table. (Hewlett-Packard managers used to call it "putting the dead rat on the table.") Placing these conversations on the table allows the sentiments to be honestly considered. In some cases they end up dissolving because they are unfounded, or ancient history, or otherwise unjustified. In other cases they are found to be valid, but once they are put on the table, they can be addressed rather than staying unspoken, where they'll only fester (or stink up the room from under the table). This process of putting unspoken sentiments on the table requires courage, and *only the top team can set the example*. However, it can be cathartic and cleansing, too. Most important, it unleashes a new sense of partnership, a sense of being "in this together," and team spirit. In addition, it elevates the leadership capacity of the team to take on much greater challenges together.

Example One

The executives at Manufacturer's Services (now part of Celestica) Arden Hills' plant did not have much respect for each other's capabilities. Only when they were able to put their views on the table were they able to shift their turnaround initiative into high gear. In a session in which heads of manufacturing, engineering, marketing, sales, and other functions expressed their displeasures with each other's competency, pent-up emotions overflowed. "Everyone who participated in it came to me afterwards and said it was the most cathartic thing they've ever been through," says Margit Elo, then VP and general manager. At the meeting, each executive had to express how he or she perceived the others. After each pronouncement, the executive on the receiving end said, "Thank you." Then the roles were reversed. The discussion surfaced many counter-productive perceptions. "They had to point out things that were getting in the way of the working relationships," Elo says.

This brutal honesty allowed the executive team to own up to their problem: that their facility was the poorest-performing one in the company, and that if it continued to lose money it would be shut down and their jobs eliminated. Quickly, the team began clicking. The defeatist, contentious culture evaporated, replaced by a culture of strong collaboration. The executives got behind Elo's initiative to make the chronically unprofitable plant profitable within 12 months. In three years, they doubled sales and became the best-performing operation in the company.

The CEO must take the lead in this step of airing hallway conversations. When she owns these unspoken conversations, she can be sincere and courageous with the leadership team and set the tone for interactions with the rest of the organization.

If team members feel the CEO lacks credibility and courage in previous initiatives, she must begin to *change that perception* immediately by admitting to past failures. This display of contrition will help to dissipate an atmosphere of insincerity and distrust.

Example Two

This was the case at Lucent's Corporate Real Estate Division. Management and its major union, the Communications Workers of America (CWA), had to come clean on previous falsehoods told by each side. "It was the standard adversarial union/management relationship," said Jim Costigan, the former president of the CWA union local. In exercises that helped both sides clear the air, union workers and Lucent executives were asked to write down what they thought of each other—and what they thought the other thought of the other.

"Management said, 'The union perceives us as being secretive and disingenuous,'" Costigan remembers. "I said, 'It's a nice word for lying.' Everyone laughed." Then a Lucent manager admitted they had told lies in the past. "A hush came to the room," Costigan recalls. Managers then explained why they felt they had to lie occasionally: The information the union often wanted from management was confidential. Experience showed that giving union people such information but asking them to keep it to themselves rarely worked. "'That's why we're secretive or at times disingenuous,' the manager said. The lightbulb went on at both sides of the room," Costigan confirms.

This meeting helped Tony Marano, head of the Real Estate Division, rebuild trust with the union. The CWA eventually agreed to workplace changes that helped cut more than $100 million in costs, reduced the expense-to-revenue ratio to 2.5 percent, increased internal customer satisfaction levels to 95 percent, and improved employee satisfaction measures to better than 80 percent.

The Picture Emerges from the Mosaic

Once context issues are satisfactorily addressed, the focus can shift to content; articulating a future for the organization. The leadership team must be aligned around a bold, compelling future in order to bring everyone else on the journey.

A key principle of generating strategic commitment is that the future an organization is envisioning and committing to is more influential on its mood, actions, and performance than its history, no matter how satisfying or disappointing that history may be. We would have never gotten a man to the moon and back by asking the engineers, scientists, and politicians to fund and deliver what they believed was possible. Great strides cannot be made by merely extrapolating the present, when 3 percent growth seems like a challenge. A mosaic of the future must be created, and it emerges only when the tiles of strategic commitment are properly installed.

There is enormous power in galvanizing people around a bold, compelling future; and that desired future state cannot be achieved by operating with yesterday's mind-set, practices, and processes. There are two ways out of this inertia: One is an externally imposed "shock to the system," such as a market or industry meltdown, a takeover by another organization, the loss of a major customer, or some other exogenous occurrence. The second is an internally generated desire to take the organization somewhere it has never been; a desire to build something extraordinary. The best leaders do the latter, because it is proactive and controllable, not reactive and random.

In Charles Savage's prescient 1990 book, *Fifth Generation Management*, he eloquently describes the difference between "clock time" and "human time." Clock time allows for a simple understanding of the past, present, and future, where the past is history and cannot be changed, and the future is something we never get to but can hope to influence. Humans relate very differently to time, however. Acting in concert within an organization we carry the past with us—sometimes in ways that are very useful and sometimes in ways that are detrimental. We also are shaped decisively by what we believe is *going to* happen. For example, if a salesperson is assigned a quota he believes is unachievable and unfair, he may remain silent in the moment because he does not want to be viewed as less than a team player. But his subsequent actions may well be driven by resentment, leading to frustration, disengagement, and ultimately less-than-optimal performance. (In a famous psychological experiment, schoolteachers who were told their class was below average finished the year with underperforming students, and those told the opposite finished with overperforming students, even though the classes comprised the same talent and test scores entering the year. For vivid examples of the effects of being trapped by diagnoses, see the 2008 book *Sway: The Irresistible Pull of Irrational Behavior*, by Ori and Rom Brafman.) For ways to "unfreeze" people's relationship with the past and the present, see Appendix, pages 10-12.

Conversely, if we are inspired by a challenge to "Beat Benz"—Lexus's rallying cry when it was first founded—we will go to extraordinary lengths to do what had previously been considered impossible, and we will often have the experience of *tempus fugit*—time flies. (And Lexus did beat Mercedes-Benz, to the point where we were called in to help create internal best practices among Mercedes dealers to beat back the threat.)

> **StratComment**
>
> *People don't rally around empty phrases and cute metaphors, no matter how memorable or clever. They rally around that which they buy into and believe, and which serves as a continuing referent point for their decisions and behaviors.*

Are You Your History or Your Future? You Really Have a Choice

Alan Kay, a former Apple Fellow, said, "The only way to predict the future is to invent it." Steve Jobs has consistently said that his strategy relies on "looking for the next big thing and jumping on it." This principle is a key part of what it takes to generate an environment of strategic commitment.

The power of a vision lies in having people genuinely believe something is possible, and by investing themselves in that vision

they behave and perform beyond what their past indicates is possible. Beliefs, after all, inform behavior. The absence of such a vision
is captured by C. K. Prahalad and Gary Hamel in their 1990 *Harvard
Business Review* "Strategic Intent" article:

> The conservative goals [that senior managers] set failed to gener-
> ate pressure and enthusiasm for competitive innovation or give the
> organization much useful guidance. Financial targets and vague
> mission statements just cannot provide the consistent direction
> that is a prerequisite for winning a global competitive war.

When people don't believe in their hearts that something is at-
tainable they will not truly invest themselves in it and go after it.
If, given their organizational culture of fear and caution, they don't
feel they can address their lack of ownership, they will either leave
(most don't!), try and change things (most will tell you that they've
tried and given up), or become numb, pretend, and go through the
motions (the most popular alternative). Watch the invidious ways in
which people go through the motions. They work hard rather than
smart; they always appear busy; they learn the "dos" and "don'ts" of
surviving and abide by them religiously.

Crafting a Bold and Compelling Future

Many companies begin formulating their strategy without addressing the hallway conversations, which is a future-threatening
mistake. Others go through the motions without addressing critical
context issues. By doing so, they dramatically curtail their ability to
have truthful, vigorous, and unconstrained dialogue on the changes
they need to make in the organization. They significantly reduce
their ability to build strategic commitment.

Mission statements, vision statements, strategic intent, purpose, credo, BHAGs (so-called big, hairy, audacious goals), and
all the labels for defining strategy, direction, and organizational

goals seem endless. And yet the poor track record of change initiatives says something is missing. To craft a bold and compelling strategy, the CEO and his team must address certain fundamental principles, not a mantra of "vision, mission, values" or a jumble of acronyms.

With respect to the *content* of the strategy, these principles are as follows:

- *The leaders must clearly and simply state the "what" of the strategy, and within what corresponding time frame.* In defining the "what" of the strategy, the leadership team must specify the results that will determine success. Answers to three categories of questions should vividly describe the firm's unique capabilities and the kind of future they are committed to building:

    1. What will we uniquely provide, deliver, or impact? What will be our unique capability and value?

    2. What will be our distinct level of quality, performance, or delivery?

    3. What kind of team will we be? What will uniquely characterize our internal culture and working dynamics?

- *Once the "what" has been established, the leadership team can begin to design the "how"—the milestones, initiatives, action plans, and accountabilities necessary for fulfilling the end state.* Too often, effective action is displaced by unproductive busy work because people are working on "how" without understanding the "what." People get consumed with monitoring and defending volumes of work without differentiating what moves things forward from that which merely fills their schedules. While "work smarter, not harder" is a familiar refrain in today's world, CEOs and their teams are often ill-equipped to make this happen.

By clearly articulating the "what" and then the "how" of the strategy, leaders focus people on outcomes, not on activities. CEOs who establish explicit direction and outcomes give people unambiguous guideposts to focus priorities. While clear direction may seem like Management 101, many organizations at all levels, even the leadership team, suffer from significant confusion about strategy and priorities.

> **StratComment**
>
> *Ends should determine means. Too many initiatives are bogged down by unnecessary inputs, activities, and tasks. Focusing on outputs, results, and deliverables will keep the means relevant and effective.*

- ◻ *The strategy must be bold enough to force the organization to be far more effective.* It must require people to stretch themselves to a new level of performance. Generating clarity alone is not sufficient; being crystal clear about a direction that will deliver merely incremental improvements will not inspire people. Organizations that achieve excellence get people to commit to a future that represents a breakthrough from the past. Their ambitious goals inspire innovation, the relentless pursuit of improvement, and a drive for success. Ritz-Carlton takes this approach, Sheraton does not. The employees reflect that difference, and the guests experience that difference.

In contrast, organizations with less ambitious goals see the starting point for next year's strategy to be this year's strategy. Improvements are incremental. They stick to the segments, territories, and opportunities they know, even though the real opportunities might be elsewhere. Lack of leadership courage produces a mood of stagnation, disappointment, and apathy throughout the organization. When strategy and the process to create it perpetuate the status quo, employees disengage.

- ◻ *Everyone must see the strategy as valid and complete.* People must understand why it is needed and (at the outset) have some idea about how they can help achieve it. They must also believe that nothing essential is missing or minimized. The strategy must be explicit enough so everyone is marching in the same direction, yet not so detailed that it prohibits individual creativity. Doing so robs people of the chance to exercise their imagination. It also undermines the need for courage because the name of the game is following—not deviating from—the rules. In Capital One's treasury department initiative, one goal was to create "strong and enduring partnerships" with the firm's lines of business. How they created such partnerships varied significantly by line of business, but the overall objective remained constant.

With respect to the *context* of the strategy, these principles must be followed:

□ *Leaders must relate to the strategic objectives as promises rather than goals.* An attitude of "we'll do our best, but if it fails we aren't responsible" almost guarantees that it will fail. By making no promises, people will feel no personal or collective risk. Getting people to promise results (i.e., achieving specific goals in a definite time frame, rather than focusing on tasks and activities) creates a much more powerful attitude.

Getting people to promise an outcome will shape the way they view the task. People will not value "working hard" to achieve the goals ("working hard" is a reflection of doing one's best). They will value "working smart." Committing to goals that require everyone to play a part, they will make sure others are succeeding and dive in if necessary. By promising results, people become interested in everything and everyone who could affect the outcome.

When Lucent/Avaya's Edison Peres asked employees to commit to grow the business tenfold in four years to $1.5 billion, everyone gulped at the goal. At first, they didn't believe it was possible. But after effectively addressing context issues, they promised each other they would achieve the goal. This helped create a culture of being an "unstoppable" team, a term that became their mantra. People worked together across regions, solved previously ignored customer problems, and followed through on items that they had dropped in the past. Four years later, they surpassed their goal, generating $1.7 billion in sales.

> □ *The executives must be in total alignment on the strategy, not merely consensus.* As we discussed in chapter 1, most CEOs attempt to get their leadership team on the same page about the direction of the organization by "building consensus." In the process, the team often must water down the new direction to one that everyone can live with, which ends up being the lowest common denominator. While this leads to consensus, it misses a higher standard—one of total alignment. Consensus elicits more a mind-set of following and going along (having no objections), especially for those whose ideas and inputs were not incorporated in the solution or direction. While people may not actively undermine the direction, they are more likely to waiver when challenged by others or circumstances. Creating consensus can make people feel like victims of the process, believing that "if they had only listened to me, we wouldn't be in this position." Furthermore, it sets the stage for excuses when events go sideways.

Team members in total alignment fully own the direction regardless of whether they had direct input into it. Total alignment can only be achieved when there is a team environment of real trust and open communication, and people can freely speculate, challenge, and subordinate their agendas for the common good. As a result, they feel like authors—not readers—of the strategy. They view bumps in the road not as reasons to exit, but as opportunities for improving the strategy.

> □ *The executive team must own the new direction uncondition-*
> *ally.* External consultants can provide valuable input into
> the content of a strategy. They can help executives see the
> current reality of the competition, the state of technologi-
> cal change, the pending impact of regulatory change, and
> how customer needs are shifting. Industry expertise and
> how to compete in it, a business process and how to design
> it, or a new information system and how to build it may
> make it necessary for the top management team to bring
> in outside help.

After all the input is taken, however, the executive team must fully own and embrace it as their creation. If they outsource the strategy completely, their challenge of generating strategic commitment significantly increases. To paraphrase famed behavioral psychologist Abraham Maslow, people will not commit to a program imposed on them by management. But they will commit to programs that they have helped create.

Note: See Appendix, page 13, for more detail on crafting a bold, compelling future.

♦ ♦ ♦

CHAPTER 4

PUSHING THROUGH THE THERMAL LAYER

How to Engage Middle Managers in Strategic Commitment

The following scenario unfolds every day in organizations of every size around the world: The CEO and the top management team unveil a strategic plan or a new initiative to dozens of executives and managers beneath them in the hierarchy. Senior management implores these mid-level managers to get on board because the initiative is critical to the success—and possibly even the survival—of the organization. After the top executives present the plan (often in a town hall–type meeting), the mid-level managers wander out into the hall, grumbling about what they just heard. The "un" and "im" words fill the air: "unrealistic," "unfathomable," "unnecessary," "unclear," "unwise," "impossible," "impractical," "unbelievable," followed by a few "whatevers."

You Can't Lead Without Light

For years, mid-level managers have been expected to endorse their companies' strategic initiatives without asking tough questions and, most of all, without dissent. Today, however, a grudging attitude of "we'll get in line even if we don't like it" is actually *worse* than outright doubt and dissent, especially for the CEO. When doubt, dissent, and resistance are overt, executives at least can take instant and corrective action. Not so when middle managers nod "yes" and think and behave in a way that says "no." It could take the CEO months if not more time to realize that the execution of the strategy is going awry. And by that time, it may be too late. A new product may be dead on arrival. A major cost-cutting program may eke out minimal savings and fail to resolve a huge pricing disadvantage. A quality improvement initiative may be too little, too late to stave off mass customer defections.

Therefore, once the leadership team has taken stock of the current reality of the organization, then crafted a compelling future and established within the executive team an environment of honest, authentic, and courageous communication, their immediate challenge is to expand the base of ownership and commitment within the next layers of management. These middle managers are pivotal because they determine the day-to-day actions and spirit of frontline employees, and breaking through this "thermal layer" to gain the commitment to a new strategy by all employees will ultimately determine whether the strategy is successful.

> **StratComment**
>
> *In every organization, the frontline people are more important for execution than the executives can ever be. A doorman makes far more of an impression on guests than the hotel manager.*

The CEO and the team begin the process by ensuring that the next layers of management see their commitment to the new direction. Leaders must address both content (especially the validity of the strategy) and context issues. Specifically, they must address the inevitable concerns (spoken or unspoken) about how this effort will differ from those of the past. Rather than whitewashing issues of doubt and skepticism, leaders must spend the time necessary to convince managers of their sincerity, courage, and concern for individuals.

Of course, the $64,000 question is: How is alignment and engagement of the middle managers rapidly accomplished?

The CEO and his leaders must be perceived as fully owning both the content and context of their strategy. They cannot delegate it to others. If people perceive that either the content or context has been "outsourced" they will quickly become cynical, lose commitment, and simply go through the motions.

In most organizations, the CEO and his leaders will spend the time creating the strategy, and in most cases the key aspects of the strategy will represent and be divided into the areas of responsibility of the key departments and functions. As a result, the senior leaders will become familiar with the content of the strategy early on and, more important, they will be identified by their managers and employees as owning those objectives that are closely related to their respective functions.

However, in many organizations external consulting firms are brought in to help with the content of the strategy, and they often have a strong influence on the content itself. It is critical, as we have indicated before—especially for the middle managers—that the CEO and his leaders always be viewed *as the owners of the strategy*. Whenever we hear the strategy being referred to as "the X consulting group strategy" it is a sure and leading indicator that an environment of strategic commitment is at risk. This is the problem with the hackneyed executive-suite plea to "Get McKinsey in here" in an attempt to secure a strategic anodyne. Too many companies, for too long, have "purchased" cookie-cutter strategies from firms that were thought to "pass muster" with the board. This is no fault of McKinsey's, but rather of executives who abdicate their responsibilities.

Avoid Strategic Limbo

Take The Hudson Bay Company as just one of many examples. For years they relied on a large consulting firm to help them create and implement their strategy. As senior executives relied more and more on the external consultants, middle management became increasingly frustrated because they felt their senior managers were abdicating ownership and accountability for the strategy to the consultants.

As Erez Weinreich, then senior vice-president of major home fashion, shared with us, "Our senior executives relied on the historic analysis of the consultants to steer the ship. People doubted the consultants' understanding of our retail business so they began to question the ability of the senior executives to turn things around. We all looked at each other and wondered why our leaders were not stepping up to lead the way. It wasn't the consultants' job to tell us how to fix our retail business, it was our own. If our leaders did not know how to fix a broken retailer, how could we expect consultants to know? We felt our leaders were refusing to lead and create a new value proposition that would fix what was ailing the company. The company was left in limbo, and everyone wanted to protect the status quo. Change was talked about, but it never happened. Politics was the flavor of the day, and the business was allowed to flounder like a rudderless ship. Executive turnover was huge. Many good executives left the company."

StratComment

Leaders who want to inspire their people to "own" the results must demonstrate that they "own" the direction, initiative, and mechanisms chosen to lead the way.

The point of these examples is not to criticize the role of the consulting groups (after all, we are consultants ourselves), but to emphasize that the CEO and top leadership team must continue to demonstrate they are the owners of the strategy throughout the process, otherwise people will disconnect themselves from the game and operate with compliance, not commitment.

Context issues are more complex from the standpoint of who owns them. In some organizations, the CEO and company leaders will say that "everyone" is responsible. However, we all know that when "everyone" is accountable "no one" is. Another very common scenario is that the CEO delegates the context issues to human resources or an outside consulting group. This is a big mistake. Why? Because it produces doubt and skepticism throughout the ranks and erodes commitment. Context issues must not appear as second in importance to the strategy and financial objectives. They must show up as a top priority. Consider the following:

- In many organizations, managers perceive the content of the strategy—the objectives and metrics—as the CEO's top priorities and the context—the culture and environment— as secondary. When managers perceive the CEO as not owning the context issues they will get discouraged and, in some cases, frustrated and resentful.

- Handing off "change management" or commitment tasks to HR erodes the leader's credibility and sincerity. The head of HR can say all she wants about the CEO's resolve, but it won't carry anywhere near the weight of the CEO demonstrating it personally. As a matter of fact, HR being the mouthpiece for the CEO sends the exact opposite mes- sage—that the CEO is not committed—and when people see that, they will disengage as well.

In a large financial institution we consulted with, a major initia- tive to articulate and immerse people in the new corporate values met with tremendous resistance when employees felt the CEO lacked a connection to the program. While dozens of training sessions involv- ing thousands of employees were conducted, with all of the ubiqui- tous supporting banners, workbooks, and takeaways for participants (including an introductory video featuring the CEO and his execu- tive committee members), cynicism nonetheless grew. No one be- lieved the CEO cared about, or owned, this enormous undertaking.

The entire exercise had been conceived, developed, promoted, and managed by human resources, which had acquired tacit approval from the executive committee. After six months of rolling out this program, several senior managers brought the intensity of the resistance to the CEO's attention. Recognizing the perceived absence of his ownership, he immediately revised the content, making it fully his own, and engaged the entire senior management group in lengthy discussions about the content of their values and the context within which they were operating.

The cynicism very rapidly transformed into shared understanding and support for the new values—unfortunately, though, significant time and resources had been lost in the process.

Engaging your managers, or employees for that matter, cannot be done by sending out a memo or slide deck; it requires the leader and his team to have a robust dialogue with middle managers about the content of the strategy and directly address context issues. HR or communications departments can and should support the creation and delivery of the content. However, the communication must come from, and be fully owned by, the leader, and it must be expressed in the CEO's own personal style. Even after the initial unveiling discussions, the CEO must have two-way dialogues with all parties to continuously update the content and address issues of context.

Managers must be told the truth about why changes are required, what the likely outcomes will be (including layoffs, if they're likely), and what will be decided at a later date. It's about full disclosure. Without it, managers will withhold their full commitment. They will resign themselves to—at best—going along with the program à la our discussion about compliance in chapter 1.

Any sign of hidden agendas, failures to disclose important facts, and outright lies, even over small issues, will diminish the trust of the leader and his team. When Steve Linehan, EVP of treasury at Capital One, was pursuing headcount and process changes for his group, he had to be direct with his team about the low probability of success around some of those changes. This candor, while not always uplifting in content, was essential in continuing to create an environment where people could deal with issues frankly, openly, and completely. Just the fact that his group knew he was committed to improving their situation, and was doing what he could to change what they considered to be long-standing difficulties, helped get people to row in behind his improvement efforts.

Offer to Listen, Then Demonstrate That You Have Listened

The CEO must exercise vigilance at this stage. The top team must not settle for mere compliance. It will only haunt them later. As they convey the new direction, managers will listen through very discriminating filters: "How will this initiative differ from previous ones?" and "Will the leadership team have the courage and resolve to address real issues this time?"

Take CHEP USA, a company that has directly addressed the context issues with its middle managers. The $3 billion pallet and container leasing company had a remarkable turnaround in operational and financial performance over a three-year period. But it had come with the pain of stretching people to much higher levels of performance. "Once you've improved the core processes that drive growth and productivity, to reach the next level of business performance you need to create very strong employee commitment," says Dave Mezzanotte, the company's former chief operating officer. "To achieve a new level of trust and communication, we addressed the context issues up-front with the middle and senior managers."

To keep managers and employees on board with the initiative, they must trust that the CEO and the top team will live up to their commitments. They must feel that if they devote themselves to this effort they will not be let down. With most large-scale change efforts, there are areas in which the CEO and his team do not have all the answers. This does not necessarily undermine commitment; that is undermined when people believe leaders lack competence but are too arrogant or insecure to admit it, ask for their help, or otherwise gain the necessary expertise.

To get his managers on board with the strategy, Mezzanotte purposefully included a broad range of managers up and down the organization in determining how to make the company's sprawling operations more efficient. He never pretended to have a grand plan that was all buttoned up. Instead, he explained that their help in coming up with the plan was essential. "It's foolish for any CEO to think he or she has all the answers," he says. "Increasingly, business leaders have to use the knowledge of the entire company to set a good direction, and make midcourse adjustments to it." Two years later, CHEP's operating and financial improvements were remarkable, including a 15 percent increase in return on capital (to 25 percent) and a $220 million increase in free cash flow.

StratComment
People need valid inclusion. It is better to have fewer meetings conducted by top people who clearly are listening than many meetings hosted by intermediaries whose listening really doesn't matter.

Besides understanding the scope and rationale of the change initiative, managers must believe they will have meaningful input and that their contributions will be valued. At the early stages of engaging everyone in the new direction, it is critical to generate a strong partnership between the leadership team and the managers.

There are, however, barriers to engaging middle managers:

- Middle managers usually carry a great deal of baggage because they've been around longest and they've seen CEOs come and go. They have known CEOs who weren't sincere, courageous, or competent enough to carry out their plans.

- They've also seen many commitments that were made and not followed through on. The more initiatives they've seen started but not completed, the more cynical they will be about the next initiative. Slogans such as "Flavor of the month" and "This too shall pass" are the clear scars of these experiences.

◻ They feel they know best what is needed, yet they are least consulted on how to do it.

◻ They often believe that voicing the most sensitive issues could get them into trouble, especially in an environment where they doubt the willingness of their leaders to face and address the real issues; they do not want to be labeled as troublemakers or as "not on board with the program."

◻ They feel unheard, unvalued, and unappreciated. They often feel those in the ivory tower are making decisions that are ignorant of the true conditions on the ground. They feel that the politics and conflicts above them force them to choose sides on issues, even when choosing sides is detrimental to operating effectively.

In addition, the CEO and leadership team often approach change in an ineffective way. For example, they dictate instead of engage, banking on clarity and relevance as the factors most influential on people's behavior. Issuing a slide deck with the key talking points of their strategy, they assume people will row in behind them because the direction has now been set and clearly articulated.

The CEO may have to own up to past false starts or failures, *even if they happened under someone else's watch.* The chief executive must recognize and acknowledge what happened and how it eroded people's faith in the firm's leadership, and then must make the case that this time around there is the commitment and competence to ensure history does not repeat itself.

Managers need to feel safe raising issues, no matter how contentious—especially about the CEO and the top team. If leaders are defensive or dismissive or act punitively, they will destroy the gains made in improving the context issues.

Involvement Is Magic

Eighteen months into Tony Marano's cost and operational improvement initiative at Lucent Real Estate, he almost squandered the strategic commitment he had built for months. In a single meeting with his top seventy-five managers to discuss the next steps in executing the productivity improvement program, he became defensive when a few managers criticized the way he was handling a personnel issue. They felt Marano had bypassed them by talking directly to their employees.

"I almost lost it," says Marano. "At first, I was irritated that people felt they could freely criticize me, their boss. But I quickly recognized that their courage to speak honestly was in fact a direct outcome of the great progress we had made in pursuing our strategic objectives. I swallowed my pride and apologized for my defensiveness." The tension in the room vanished quickly, and his managers' frustration dissipated. Everyone was once again prepared to listen with interest to what Marano was saying. In the end, this nearly disastrous incident actually strengthened the team's commitment to the improvement program.

> **StratComment**
>
> *Checking your ego at the door can make more space for other people to enter the room.*

In 2003, the way Steve Linehan got his beleaguered staff at Capital One to get behind a two-year plan to significantly improve treasury performance was to speak plainly about the challenging working conditions within the group and take meaningful actions to improve them. His associates were far less concerned about the way he expressed his plan, and far more concerned that he recognized and understood their issues.

"People in this business are way too smart for corporate-speak," Linehan says. "They want honest, from-the-gut answers. You'll lose them with anything else." Over the next twelve months, his function's environment and performance improved dramatically. Associates worked hard to "fortify funding" (one key area of focus). They bolstered processes and risk management controls, and worked closely with external investor groups. Over time, this helped Capital One achieve an upgraded investment rating and significantly decrease cash management costs.

When middle managers are engaged effectively, it is magical. It unleashes a level of energy and excitement throughout the organization—a "buzz"—and generates an environment of unmistakable ownership, commitment, and accountability.

For Tony Marano at Lucent, getting the middle managers on board was viewed as an exceedingly difficult challenge. Most were twenty-five-year veterans of the Bell System, known as crusty, old-school, command-and-control managers who had survived by being tougher than the union leaders they confronted daily about overtime, work assignments, and grievances.

Marano's leadership team told us that we would never confront a group this difficult: "These guys have no time or tolerance for any kind of happy talk." Their toughness was only a reflection of how committed they were to making things work, and how frustrated and resigned they had become; these folks had seen and been through it all. After they had a chance to voice their heartfelt concerns, and felt genuinely listened to and heard by Marano and his executive team, their strong cynicism melted and they completely dropped their guard. They became some of the staunchest supporters of Marano's efforts to make significant cost and operational improvements. Their shift in mind-set and behavior sent an indelible signal to the frontline supervisors and employees that this effort was for real, and that being a bystander was not a viable position.

Jim Burns (names in this example are fictional), managing director of the U.K. region for a large global telecommunications company, needed to transform his organization—the second largest in the company's operations—to be able to continue to achieve the company's aggressive growth expectations in a time of challenging economics and growing competition in his market. After an impressive six-year run of consistently meeting or exceeding expectations through a very tightly controlled and hands-on management style, down to managing revenue commitments on a weekly basis, Burns realized that the only way to take his tremendously successful organization to the next level was to create a new level of personal ownership and accountability throughout his management ranks.

According to Burns: "We have very talented leaders and managers. However, continuing to maintain our track record was becoming more and more strenuous on me personally. I felt I couldn't step back from driving the daily activities because I wasn't confident that without my direct oversight, my managers would operate with the same level of ownership and accountability as I have to ensure we meet every week's commitment, with no glitches and excuses. As a result, I often had to step in when I felt things were getting out of hand. This was a suboptimal and frustrating dynamic for my managers and me. I was frustrated that they weren't stepping up, and they were getting frustrated that I wasn't letting them run their businesses. Even though we were very successful, I only realized later how high the negative sentiments actually were."

After acknowledging and addressing the context issues, including putting the hallway conversations on the table and getting on the same page about the new direction and standards of performance required for taking the U.K. region to the next level, the entire leadership team fully embraced Burns's intent. The department heads started to work together at a new level and the team began to address the issues that were slowing them down. One of the areas of frustration was related to the fact that the workweek started on Monday. As Bob Kernan, VP of sales, explained, "This meant that people often had to work on the weekends to ensure that all the orders went through, and this was hurting their work-life balance. So we decided to change our week cycle from Monday through Sunday to Friday through Thursday. While being a simple thing, it was a significant change for us because, as a result, all orders were fulfilled by Thursday, Fridays were used to fore-cast and plan for the week, and people were able to stop working on the weekends. Everyone started to feel much more empowered and excited to drive our business, and Jim was able to pull out more and focus on bigger, more strategic things." According to Kernan, this is just one example of the changes that they have made since they took on the aggressive game plan that Burns was undertaking.

Why Slow Is Fast

Within his treasury function, Steve Linehan met frequently with his senior and middle managers to encourage and support them in owning the content and context of their initiative. Al Ciafre, then director of securitization for Capital One's Auto franchise, took the initiative to gather his team and craft a "mini-vision" for their unit, establish success criteria and action plans to reach those criteria, and address all context issues within his team on an ongoing basis. While Linehan could have dictated that each of his managers take these steps, *it was much more powerful and effective for each of them to embrace the principles of generating strategic commitment and design an approach that would fit within their respective areas.* Linehan's resolve that they do so was unwavering; his willingness for them to tailor for local is-sues and concerns was empowering.

In so many organizations the CEO does not have the patience, understanding, or willingness to invest the time and effort to ensure a solid foundation of commitment is in place. When asked, a senior ex-ecutive in a leading global telecommunications company said, "The business is moving so fast we don't have the time to deal with context issues." But this is exactly the fatal mistake leaders make. When it comes to generating an environment of strategic commitment, slow is fast. The CEO and his leaders have to do it right, otherwise they'll have to deal with the lack of a strong foundation for strategic commitment throughout the entire journey. Instead of building a strong foundation for outstanding performance, these leaders settle for compliance, and when things don't work out well, they pay a premium in terms of rework and inefficiencies.

Here's a typical example: Within a $1 billion professional services firm we worked with, the CEO was receiving continual feedback regarding the dysfunctional traits of his leadership team. Executives were afraid to speak up, and there was an overall feeling that this was a very political and fragmented environment in which everyone looked out for himself.

> **StratComment**
> *Taking the time to gain strategic commitment pays off; a slower start ensures a faster finish.*

Despite the feedback about these significant context issues, the CEO forged ahead with a sweeping improvement initiative involving the entire management group. People believed it was a critical undertaking in order to improve the ailing profitability of the firm, especially given the fact that the market was taking a turn for the worse after being very high the years before. However, they engaged reluctantly because of their significant doubts about the CEO's level of courage and resolve to really hear, own, and address the tough issues. With significant fanfare and assignment of resources to the improvement initiative, minimal improvements were realized, but they did not live up to the full expectations. More worrisome was the fact that throughout this multiyear process the dysfunctional dynamics became worse, increasing the cynicism among top leadership.

The leaders blamed the limited progress on the CEO's lack of courage and resolve, while the CEO felt it was because of the market conditions and lack of ownership among his leaders. We unfortunately still observe this dynamic, or variations on it, in many organizations.

Getting managers at all levels to truly commit to the strategy is a major milestone in the change initiative. The CEO must give managers the tools with which they can create the same dynamics within the employee population. To do that, *managers must adhere to the same principles of addressing both content and context issues with their people.* They must ensure employees clearly understand the validity of the new strategy—its content—and how their jobs and functions contribute to it and support it in the long term.

A word of caution: Even after the middle managers are on board, the CEO and his team cannot and must not stop leading from the front. They must always be readily seen, atop the horse, leading the way into the battle.

CHAPTER 5

♦ ♦ ♦

LEADING FROM THE FRONT

"Follow Me!" (Not, "I'll Be There in a Minute . . .")

Every organization is a reflection of its leadership. More specifically, every organization is only as strong or as weak as its leaders. Hence, if CEOs want to bring about change they must start at the top—personally and then with their direct reports.

If you don't believe this to be inexorably true, consider the dynamic and almost metaphysical turnarounds, positive and negative, at IBM under Lou Gerstner; Hewlett-Packard under Carly Fiorina; Merck under Ray Gilmartin; Apple under John Sculley (and then Steve Jobs); HealthSouth under Richard Scrushy; Alcatel-Lucent under Patricia Russo; the city of Washington, D. C., under Mayor Marion Barry; the army under Ulysses S. Grant; and New York City's infrastructure development under Robert Moses.

One person does make the difference, even in complex, heterogeneous, and political organizations.

When you learn to be an officer in the military, "leading from the front" is a very clear, straightforward, ingrained discipline. And when you go into combat you learn very quickly, and firsthand, that when the time comes to charge, your people will rush in only if they trust that you will be there in the front: "Follow me!" not "I'll be there in a minute." In business, even though one could make the valid case that lives are not at stake in the same way they are in combat, we believe that the companies that have become the most powerful and successful are those that bring the same level of passion, commitment, and accountability to the game—*as if lives are at stake*. In order to generate the power of strategic commitment the CEO must "lead from the front."

The most powerful and inspiring CEOs are those who truly hold themselves accountable for everything—and they consider it a privilege, not a burden or obligation. When things go well they give the credit to others, and when things go badly they take personal responsibility. They look to see where they can provide greater leadership in direction, demand for excellence, or inspiration and motivation in order to correct things and elevate their teams. They view the orientation around blame and fault as cancerous, so when things go wrong they avoid asking "Who's fault is it?" and orient themselves and their people only around conversations that make a difference: "What's missing?" "What's in the way?" "What needs to be corrected?" and "What can we learn from this?" In short, they seek *cause, not blame*. They understand that the most important thing to do with bad past events is to learn as much as possible from them (otherwise, by default, these bad events become the excuses and justifications for excessive caution, leading to reduced future performance).

Powerful CEOs view other people's elevation and achievements as their own personal achievement, hence, they are oriented around motivating, elevating, empowering, coaching, and developing people. They are not threatened by others' successes or stature. They put their egos aside and see their mission in life as achieving great results though extremely empowered people. And this keeps them humble. The role of leaders should be to develop their successors, and their true test is if they are able to develop leaders around them who are greater and stronger than they are. From our combined experience, however, we have found this to be the exception not the rule. Far more prevalent are managers and employees who feel their ability to step up and grow is limited because superiors feel threatened by their growing stature. (For a great historical example, see *Team of Rivals*, by Doris Kearns Goodwin, about Lincoln's ability to share credit, take blame, and create common cause for otherwise antithetical interests.)

Taking on real change is like signing a blank check. It is a wholehearted commitment without knowing in advance everything it is going to entail—what we refer to as an "unconditional" commitment. (We will expand on this principle in the next chapter.)

> **StratComment**
>
> *"Leader" and "exemplar" are really inseparable descriptions. If a leader isn't exemplifying the behaviors, values, and results cherished in the organization, then that leader will fail and is a failure.*

A change initiative is a personal commitment for the CEO; so before taking it on, the CEO should ask a series of key questions to determine if she is truly committed and ready for the journey:

- Do I have a clear sense of where I am headed? Do I know where I want to be, even if I don't yet know how to get there?

- Am I convinced that the way it is today is not good enough?

- Do I have what it takes to follow through, no matter how difficult, messy, and uncomfortable it may get? Do I have the courage, the patience, and the energy?

- Will I doubt, second-guess, or reduce my passion when things become turbulent?

- Will I give up and allow the initiative to fall between the cracks when the going gets tough or the results don't show up fast enough?

- Will I stay the course even if it is uncomfortable or I look bad for a while and feel inadequate along the way?

(Recall that Warren Buffett was called "too old" and "out of touch" when he refused to take part in the technology bubble, which he correctly predicted would crash.) Or will I come up with excuses, reasons, and stories when things get tough?

- Do I have tolerance for things to get worse before they get better (in change initiatives this is often the case)?

- Will I commit to driving the desired business results by engaging, inspiring, empowering, and motivating people?

- Will I commit to generating an environment of open, honest, and real communication? Will I support an environment where people tell the truth (no lip service and lies) and give honest feedback even about the tough subjects, including about my leaders and me, and where commitment not compliance is the standard? Or will I only be open when there is good news, which will inevitably breed silos, politics, and fear?

- Will I dedicate the time and effort to mentor, coach, and elevate my leaders?

- Will I invest the time and effort to engage my organization, and ensure my people experience me as available, accessible, and feel my presence?

- Will I commit to leading from the front and always taking the view that I am the source of the good and bad things that are happening in this organization? Or will I blame others and circumstances when things don't go well?

- Will I make clear declarations and put my reputation on the line with my own superiors and the board about where I'm headed and how I'll lead to get there?

Let's explore this topic further.

The Résumé of the Senior Leadership Team: Ten Essential Leadership Competencies and Qualities

The senior leadership team must also do the same—hold themselves accountable for leading from the front and leading by example, thereby being powerful role models. It doesn't matter what people read and hear, because they will watch how the CEO and top team members are behaving and will take their cues from them.

Doubts about their leader's individual or collective sincerity, courage, competence, or concern for the workforce will undermine people's commitment. You can't proclaim that you are supporting the organization's value that the customer is supreme if you refuse to take customers' calls. In a notoriously egregious example, one CEO pushed his executives to buy into a cost-cutting program while simultaneously spending several hundred thousand dollars on a private exercise room in the office adjacent to his own. No wonder he was having trouble getting people to take the cost-cutting campaign seriously. While this may be an extreme case, it is not at all unusual for managers to view their leaders as hypocrites when they are facing cost-cutting mandates yet see their leaders continuing to spend on events, entertainment, and even office upgrades that appear extravagant.

There are ten leadership qualities and competencies that leaders must individually and collectively internalize and demonstrate to meet this challenge. They are listed in Figure 5-1 and will be discussed, one by one, in the following sections. See also Appendix, page 234.

Orient Around Making a Difference, Rather Than Protecting Ego and Status

Leaders must focus on empowering and making a difference with their team and beyond, rather than on their own career path,

1. Orient around making a difference, rather than protecting ego and status.

2. Make the vision come alive in a meaningful way.

3. Be authentic.

4. Operate with integrity.

5. Act with boldness and courage.

6. Have other's backs unconditionally.

7. Communicate openly and honestly.

8. Generate passion, energy, and enthusiasm.

9. Build and empower leaders around them.

10. Be committed to development and growth.

Figure 5-1. Leadership competencies and qualities.

compensation, status, or ego. They need to be *interested* in, and fully invested in, making others around them successful rather than focusing on themselves. They need to identify themselves with the success of their people and the company, rather than their own personal agenda.

Strong leadership teams enable people to participate in a common cause and, by doing so, to see themselves as part of a shared identity. Leadership transforms individuals into active members of a broader collective entity. Leaders have the capacity to appropriately position their personal ego and concerns relative to the needs of the larger environment in which they are operating. Leadership is not about saying, "Hey, look at what a great leader I am." It is about enabling the achievement of a greater overall good that would not have been possible without their direct involvement, but without their needing to stand up and take credit for that accomplishment. In this sense, leadership is not about "me" or "us," it is about "them".

A leadership team's greatest obligation is to cultivate an environment where people's minds and hearts can be fully engaged in the organization's mission, where people can aspire to do useful and significant things, where people can aspire to change the world. If you listen to the flavor of conversations among successful, inspired leadership teams, you will often hear them talk about their organization as a place where talented and motivated people want to come because they believe it will be a place where they can change the world.

Leaders do not view strategy and execution as abstract concepts, but as elements that are ultimately about people. Leaders are not focused on themselves, but on the people who they are trying to inspire by unleashing their talents, their hopes, and their aspirations. They relate to themselves as levers helping their people succeed, rather than viewing their people as instruments to advance personal agendas. As Henry Mintzberg said, "Strategy and planning don't make things happen. People do."

Make the Vision Come Alive in a Meaningful Way

Strong leaders are clear about—and make vivid—their vision, commitment, and stand. They ensure their vision and commitments are present in a meaningful way and are guiding and inspiring all actions and behaviors, shaping people's passion, focus, or priorities, not merely sitting in drawers or hanging as memos in people's cubicles. They make sure the vision is alive in the day-to-day dialogues of the organization, both for tactical and strategic issues, and that it really is the guiding light for decision making and choices about time, resources, and budgets.

Strong leadership teams declare a future state and manage present-day activities and interactions from and toward that future state—so they cause that future to come to fruition through every interaction and activity. This is about much more than simply establishing a set of objectives; it is about making that future state their personal mission, and passionately and relentlessly driving the organization to realize it.

Declaring a future, as we will talk more about in chapter 6, is about letting people know what you stand for and what you are building. It's about putting yourself out there, making yourself vulnerable to risk of failure. This orientation creates a sense of ownership for the journey and the collective commitment to accomplishing the outcome. It creates the energy required to complete the journey and to accomplish the objectives.

Be Authentic

Authenticity in all communications and interactions is essential. Leadership must be transparent, with the leaders committed to what they say, with no hidden agendas. They must represent themselves without bravado, without self-promotion, and without exaggeration. They must stand tall for what they believe in, and be unwavering about principles. In addition, they must own up to shortcomings without sugar-coating or rounding the corners related to shortfalls or missteps. Executives who attempt to soft-pedal bad news by trying to offset it with good news are insulting people by treating them like children. When mistakes are made, or when tough measures are called for, people appreciate being told the truth, the potential impact on them, and what is needed from them in order to help move things forward. Executive teams that avoid these types of interactions with their people quickly lose respect and confidence.

Authenticity must start at home, within the leadership team. How they interact with each other affects how they interact with—and how they will be perceived by—everyone else.

Operate with Integrity

It doesn't take a rocket scientist to understand that people will not follow someone they don't trust. People need to know their leaders can be trusted, that they are ethical, and that they will be honest in their dealings. Without trust, grand visions and bold declarations will be received as egomaniacal chest-thumping and will be ignored. Until people believe leaders will be true to their word, genuine followership will be impossible. While people may feel compelled to follow their leaders due to organizational or hierarchical politics and fear, their actions will, at best, be far more a function of compliance than authentic commitment. To this end, leaders must be vigilant about following through on the commitments they make, and they must acknowledge and take responsibility for screw-ups when they occur (as they inevitably will in any organization seeking to lead the pack).

All commitments, large and small, must be consistently managed, tracked, and followed through. This is no small task. People often say one thing and do another, rather than clarify what they promise and thoroughly account for those promises. No wonder people commonly refer to talk as cheap. Without follow-through, people will conclude that leadership is insincere or lacks resolve or competence. We have seen initiatives loudly proclaimed on January 1 that are all but forgotten by June 30 because the senior team is overwhelmed with competitive actions, economic changes, politics, organizational resistance, and so on.

People also need to know that when tested, their leaders will live up to the values and principles they have declared. Not because anyone is watching, but because they have an inner compass that they can rely on when the easy answers cease to exist.

Act with Boldness and Courage

Strong leaders are guided by their vision and commitment, not their fears, doubts, uncertainties, or comfort zones. They are not immune from fears, doubts, and uncertainties, to be sure, but they are not paralyzed by them. They are willing to push the envelope in their own communications and actions for the good of their vision and commitment.

People need to know their leaders will not falter when times get tough. That they will not take the easy way out or let themselves off the hook for the journey they have embarked upon. People need to feel their leaders will back them up and not leave them hanging when they encounter the inevitable turbulence associated with pursuing meaningful objectives, or when things get worse before getting better.

People need leaders who will face reality and address the difficult and contentious issues without flinching, or making excuses, or finding easily accepted explanations and rationalizations when the truth is more difficult to swallow.

People also need to know their leaders will do the right thing based on mutually agreed principles and not fall back or look for the easy ways out. Doing what is necessary will not always be easy or popular. Having *courage* means saying what you stand for and having the resolve to stay the course when encountering the inevitable adversity a bold undertaking provokes. *Boldness* means having the will to act and the resolve to follow through. It means going beyond the rhetoric and the speculation and acting while others are still contemplating and debating available options.

Leaders could be separated into two categories in this arena. First, there are the cautious ones who are oriented around being careful and being comfortable with things working well as they are. "It seems to work fine . . . we've been really successful at it . . . it's the industry standard operating procedure . . . it's too risky to rock the boat, so let's not change it." The highest criteria for success for these leaders is meeting or beating other companies' benchmarks. The second category is leaders who are oriented around thinking that says, "Let's see how great we can be!" These leaders are *informed* by others' benchmarks, but are constantly pushing the envelope—rocking the boat when necessary—to set and achieve their own standards of ever-greater performance and results. They are constantly looking at how to apply boldness and innovation for organizational improvement, rather than for its own sake. The possibility of coming up with something truly transformational makes challenging the status quo well worth the risk of failure and separates the caretakers from those who will inspire their organizations to accomplish something significant.

Have Others' Backs Unconditionally

Leaders represent their peers as partners at all times because they genuinely feel and believe it. They are committed to each other and feel others are committed to them. They do not tolerate behind-the-back conversations of any kind that undermine their partners; triangulation is unacceptable. If one team member has an issue with another, they sit down together and deal with it openly, directly, and rapidly. There is no time to waste because the future is at stake. They are focused on building an environment of genuine trust, integrity, and credibility, knowing that only by them living this behavior can they expect their people to do the same.

They take responsibility for how they are perceived collectively and individually. They make sure their team members experience them as open, honest, trusting, authentic, courageous, and committed, and that stakeholders experience the team as a cohesive, honest, courageous, authentic, caring team that lives up to its vision and commitments.

When leaders unconditionally have each other's backs, they are able to have blunt, direct, tough conversations about difficult tactical, strategic, operational, and personal challenges, and they always trust that they will reach a state of true alignment that will be reflected in a unified voice. Because they own each other's success, they feel comfortable holding each other to account and calling each other out when colleagues, including their CEO, are not living up to their commitments, but they also acknowledge their fellow leaders when they are performing well as exemplars.

Communicate Openly and Honestly

Leaders always communicate openly, authentically, and courageously. They never leave conversations and communication undelivered or incomplete. They understand that splinters of communication left unattended become gangrenous; they therefore place a premium on raising and addressing any and all misunderstandings, rumors, gossip, or hallway talk that could in any way undermine the future they are collectively committed to. Once again, they have zero tolerance for behind-the-back conversations of any kind.

They also provide feedback and coaching to each other, including their CEO. And they are genuinely open and willing to receive and accept open, honest, and even blunt feedback, no matter how uncomfortable it may feel.

While not always the case, we often find strong social bonds within effective leadership teams. A bond builds among team members who have committed to a bold future, and the social activities they partake in strengthen their ability to deal directly with difficult issues back at work. They become more and more aware of their colleagues' preferences, styles, and idiosyncrasies, all of which supports their ability to communicate without reservations.

Generate Passion, Energy, and Enthusiasm

Leaders inspire and motivate others and are inspired and motivated by others. They understand the power of energy, and they consider it their direct responsibility to continuously infuse the organization with passion, energy, and enthusiasm. Different leaders have different styles, whether introverted and analytical or outgoing and charismatic. No particular style is a prerequisite and no particular style makes generating passion, energy, and enthusiasm impossible. (This observation runs counter to conventional wisdom, which says that you must be a charismatic leader to inspire others to follow.)

Passion is about the leaders fully identifying themselves with the future of the organization. It is about believing in the mission and direction so much that they figuratively *become* the mission. This conviction is contagious, and it allows others to get energized by their enthusiasm.

Purpose and passion go hand in hand. It starts with caring deeply about the mission and the people on the mission. It is a passion for a higher purpose that is characterized by being open to possibilities, and the innate belief that people want to work together to create the best future imaginable.

Passion is also about demanding excellence. Without passion, one can nitpick or become a perfectionist; with passion, this quality is transformed into a commitment for others to elevate themselves to ever-higher standards of performance.

Strong leaders share a fundamental belief that there is nothing a highly motivated workforce cannot achieve given the right tools and resources. They know that capital equipment and raw materials are (to some extent) commodities; the real differentiator is building a team of people who have the desire and drive to overcome whatever might impede a competitor.

Build and Empower Leaders Around Them

Leaders must be able to motivate others to act through influence and inspiration rather than fear and authority. If they resort to authority they will not have thinkers and partners on the journey, but rather people who need to be policed or disciplined to ensure they stay on course. Declaring what a team stands for creates influence, inspiration, and thinkers.

Leadership teams need to be focused on creating a pipeline of new leaders around them who can build the future of the organization. It is one of the most essential competencies because it assures that the company will always have skilled and prepared people to lead it well into the future.

This in no way means that leaders should abdicate their responsibilities. In fact, empowering and enabling others demands even more attention and diligence. You cannot assume that people are going to succeed and therefore you just leave them alone to do it themselves. Rather, you must take full responsibility for ensuring their success.

Key to success in creating and managing a leadership pipeline is the development of a coaching/mentoring mind-set that is focused on enabling others to lead. To this end, leaders must treat every interaction as an opportunity to foster, cultivate, demand, and encourage others to elevate themselves in the leadership domain. An important aim here is to build self-confidence by encouraging, caring for, and recognizing progress. Self-confidence energizes and gives people the courage to stretch, take risks, and do things they never thought they could before. These activities and this orientation cannot be restricted to leadership programs or formal coaching sessions. In fact, these tools may be less effective ways to develop leaders. It's a mind-set that looks for frequent and continuous "coachable" moments focused on leadership.

As a leadership team, it is making "our" success about "their" success, and paying attention to, and caring for, those who are on the journey with us. This is not about being soft and mushy with people, nor about avoiding having tough conversations. It is about knowing that people are big, and mature, and capable, and dealing with them from the perspective that they can learn and grow by directly facing difficult issues. It means giving meaningful and honest feedback about where people stand without rounding the corners or being so concerned about giving a balanced message that people are left believing they are in better shape than you believe they are.

Be Committed to Development and Growth

Leaders are constantly working to push themselves and their team to the next level, even when it means addressing and tackling barriers and tough topics to do so. They never avoid issues, no matter how sensitive or uncomfortable they are. This commitment to growth includes being open, compassionate, and humble. As others have commented:

> "The more I learn, the more I realize I don't know and the more
> I want to learn."
> Albert Einstein

> "When you are an individual contributor you try to have all the answers. When you are a leader, your job is to have all the questions. You have to be incredibly comfortable looking like the dumbest person in the room."
> Jack Welch

The best leaders are those who welcome advice and admit they don't have all the answers. The leader who knows his strengths and weaknesses is likely to be far more effective than the one who remains blind to them.

Some leaders are so wrapped up in the notion that they are supposed to know everything that they fail to study and understand their strengths and weaknesses. They fall into the trap of trying to lead an organization in an evolving world without actually evolving themselves. They make decisions based on old knowledge, assumptions, and habits. They fall into a rut and wind up repeating past mistakes and missing key opportunities.

Understanding one's strengths and weaknesses creates a great opportunity to grow as a leader. If the leader stops growing, then the organization stops growing as well. Organizations with leaders who openly understand and develop their strengths and weaknesses create an environment where everyone else will do the same. As the leader grows, so grow the people, and as people grow, so grows the organization.

If you want your people to experiment and learn, you need to set the example. You will make them feel more comfortable about exploring their own opportunities for development. As they see you make progress, they can start to envision their own progress. The leaders of an organization set the tone for how personal development is viewed. This means not letting themselves off the hook with platitudes such as, "Well, we all have areas where we can improve."

Humility is one of those leadership traits often perceived as a weakness when, in fact, it can be a tremendous asset. Humble leaders rarely allow the power of their position to cloud their judgment. Leaders who recognize they are not perfect create an environment where those around them feel comfortable making mistakes and taking chances. Humble leaders assume that they do not know all the answers and allow people to explain things to them. They look for the opportunity to learn something new, and they use every opportunity to make others feel valued. The humble leader knows the world around her is changing faster than she can keep up and is grateful for the opportunity to learn something new or reinforce knowledge she might already possess.

StratComment

Anonymous feedback is safe, but candid, direct feedback is far more efficacious. The former reflects top teams that don't trust each other, and the latter exemplifies those teams whose members put personal and collegial growth above all else.

Leadership is also about understanding, empathy, and being able to relate to and connect with those you are asking to engage with you. People will not follow without feeling heard, valued, and cared for. People want to matter, they want to make a difference, and they want to be known for their contributions.

The behavior of its leaders will either inspire the organization or hinder its spirit and performance. While this would seem to be self-evident, we are constantly surprised by CEOs' blindness to the impact of their behavior (what they do and don't do, and how they do it) on their organizations and people.

A seasoned executive at a Fortune 100 company had a habit of frequently working his BlackBerry while in meetings. He hired us to help him generate an environment of strategic commitment within his department as they were entering a very difficult business environment that required downsizing and improvements in customer satisfaction at the same time. As we were preparing for our initial meeting with him, we asked some of his leaders to tell us about him. The overall feedback was that he was a competent, knowledgeable leader, yet somewhat uncaring and at times disrespectful. Based on people's descriptions, we entered the meeting with concerns about the sincerity of his intentions.

During our meeting he checked his BlackBerry every few minutes. At one point we asked him if he had to deal with an urgent matter; his reply was a casual "no." So we continued. After he again looked at his device a few times we stopped the meeting and pointed out to him that he seemed distracted. He was quite surprised and embarrassed; he was quite unaware of the negative impact of his behavior on others. We then shared with him some of the feedback we had received about him from his colleagues, and it became quite obvious that people were interpreting his behavior as showing a lack of respect for them. When he realized the impact of this behavior on his people, he immediately took it upon himself to stop it and apologized as appropriate. And—in a very short period of time—the hallway conversations started to change from "He doesn't care" to "He's a very caring and committed leader." We see similar examples everywhere.

How Leadership Behavior Has Changed to Less Leadership

It was tough to be a brigadier general in 1863. The highest rate of casualties as a percentage of rank in the American Civil War was among brigadier generals, because they were out front, leading their brigade forward while seated on a horse. Every enemy sharpshooter aimed for the leader. It became common in modern wars for officers to remove their insignia, so as not to draw fire on themselves. And in contemporary warfare—due to advances in technology rather than any lack of leadership or courage—it is extraordinarily rare for a general officer to be killed by enemy fire, because they are in bunkers to the rear or not even in the vicinity.

Deaths among high-ranking firefighters are common, because unlike the police department's operating procedure of having ranking officers stand back to manage dangerous developments, the fire department's credo is that senior officers lead their men and women into the danger. You would be hard-pressed to find a high-ranking fire department officer about whom it could be said, "He was never in harm's way."

Ergo, leaders must constantly set the example.

In another setting, John Weaver, then general manager of Augusta Newsprint Company, aligned his leadership team around a vision of being "Top Ten in the World" within their industry. Ranked forty-ninth (out of more than 500) at the outset, he was anxious to get his 400 employees on board as quickly as possible. Recognizing that dealing with context issues was the entry point to a more productive and effective workforce, he gathered a group of supervisors and shop stewards to begin to gain their alignment. After sharing the overall intent of the new vision, this unforgettable exchange took place:

> **Weaver:** I'm happy to share this new vision with you. I know everyone in this room is key to making this happen. I'd like your input on how best we can make this happen, which includes letting me know if there are things we are doing that are in the way.
> **Shop Steward:** Do you really want to know what's in the way?
> **Weaver:** Yes, absolutely.
> **SS:** You sure you want to hear it?
> **Weaver:** Definitely.
> **SS:** Can we tell the truth in here?
> **Weaver:** Without question.
> **SS:** The problem is that everyone on the shop floor thinks you're an asshole. [Gasps are heard!]

Weaver: How come?

SS: Because every morning when you walk through the plant people say hello to you, but you never respond.

Weaver [after a long pause]: You know, come to think of it, I always park my car out back, then I walk in the back door through the manufacturing area [which is as loud as a locomotive], go to my office, and the first thing I do is put in my hearing aid. [Laughter erupts.] The reason I don't respond is because I can barely hear without my hearing aid. From now on, if any of you say hello to me and I don't respond, I want you to come over and wave in my face. I promise I'll make a point of saying hello.

This interaction was one of many that helped to establish a platform of trust, respect, and open communication within the operation. Within two years, they succeeded in joining the ranks of the top-ten newsprint operations in the world. And, as an aside, Weaver shortly thereafter became a member of the executive committee and went on to become president and chief executive officer of the parent company five years later.

Carl Peterson (name fictionalized), a senior director at a multinational pharmaceutical company, was well known as a brilliant, visionary strategist, an industry expert, and the recipient of numerous industry awards for sales programs. As brilliant as he was, he was also viewed as inflexible and stubborn ("my way or the highway"). Even within his own team, people often felt intimidated by him. He was not fond of halfbaked ideas; he challenged people quickly and left them feeling they could not match his level of intellect. While his organization's results were impressive and the programs he designed received accolades, the levels of frustration within his team and among his peers were rising steadily. Initially, Peterson's strongly held view was that he was the guardian of these programs and that others' frustrations with his

> **StratComment**
>
> *Perhaps most leaders need to learn how to make sure their "hearing aid" is in place and turned on every morning, even if their normal hearing is just fine.*

style were irrelevant. It took some time, but eventually he recognized the severity of people's sentiments and the degree to which those sentiments were weakening his stakeholders' engagement with his programs. When he realized his stakeholders were avoiding coming to him with issues, and instead were looking for ways to go around him, he committed to change his behavior and thereby improve his effectiveness. He spent much more time with his team and his stakeholders building alignment and understanding, which resulted in increased partnership and collaboration. While he had always been successful, the personal changes he made allowed for dramatic improvements in program effectiveness, leading to significantly higher revenues from the products he managed.

There are, however, leadership attributes that CEOs consider as strengths but are in fact detrimental to generating strategic commitment.

Why the Trusted Few Can't Be Trusted

Much of management literature on leadership gives executives wrongheaded ideas about how to generate commitment. Being the *sole visionary* can be one. When the leader believes his role is to be lead visionary at the company that can be taken to its logical excess: feeling responsible for coming up with all the details of the strategy, or overcontrolling the strategic process or product. As a consequence, the leader will exclude others from shaping the strategy without even noticing it. That will discourage people from embracing the strategy and, in the end, will produce mere compliance.

Leaders often believe that too many participants will prolong the process and dilute the clarity, validity, and relevance of the work product. Therefore, they put the creation of the content of the strategy in the hands of a trusted few (often the strategy group, the heads of the lines of business, or a select group of confidants) and share the final product with all those charged with execution only when it is done or almost done. (A senior vice president at the Associated Press patiently explained to us many years ago that executives "would *never* involve too many people in our strategy process, or even show them the result. That would be irresponsible!" You can't make this stuff up.)

The CEO of a large services firm we worked with, for example, believed that the optimal-size group should be five, which included the heads of his five business lines, and that the heads of the support functions should be excluded. His strong belief was that the HR, IT, Finance, and Legal department managers would have little to offer in the strategy conversation and, in fact, would impede progress. Over time, however, he became frustrated that the strategy was being implemented too slowly.

This CEO's attitude is quite common. Such executives fail to realize the downside of keeping strategy development an exclusive process. The faster they generate the content, the slower they will resolve the context issues (again, fast is slow). Those who are excluded from the process feel disrespected. They find it hard to support the decisions, even if they don't express these sentiments. They view the strategy as "theirs" and not "mine" (even if, had they been included, they would have agreed with it). Furthermore, a tightly controlled strategy process discounts the expertise these senior professionals could offer to ensure the content of the strategy passes the litmus tests of validity and relevance across the broadest possible spectrum of constituents. The CEO mentioned above added the heads of the support functions to his strategy development team after realizing that they could make significant contributions. That sent a message to the organization that all functions were important and therefore the strategy development process was becoming more inclusive.

> **StratComment**
>
> *Leading and listening are complementary, not antithetical. Leadership is enhanced, not diminished, by listening to all viewpoints. In fact, the best ideas usually come from integrating perspectives gained by dealing directly with the customers, stakeholders, and employees.*

Excluding executives from strategy development also undermines the ability of the leadership team to operate with a shared purpose, which will become immediately evident to lower-level managers and employees. Leaders and managers will appear insincere and lacking in resolve. In turn, that will slow down the pace of adoption.

Every leader knows that *supreme confidence* is a key leadership trait for generating commitment. Yet in reality it can often undermine commitment. Leaders can unconsciously send signals that they have all the answers or aren't open to input or criticism. If people feel they can't contribute they will become frustrated, disengage, and often adopt a resentful attitude: "We'll let them hang themselves." This is fatal for CEOs because the minute something unexpected happens during execution—which we have pointed out is inevitable, given the pace of change—people will pretend they are trying to fix the situation when in fact they will have adopted the "I told you so" and "serves them right" attitude.

Another problem occurs when leaders have strong views about the direction of the organization yet instead of sharing them and enrolling their people, they try to steer people toward coming up with this direction on their own. In this case the leader appears to be seeking consensus when in fact the leader's mind is made up in advance. This is transparently manipulative, like the old "eight of clubs" trick. (You drive the other person to select the card in your hand, the eight of clubs, through manipulative questioning. "Choose two suits," you say. "Hearts and diamonds," they respond. "That leaves clubs and spades, choose one of them." You get the picture.) Once people begin to feel manipulated into something that has already been decided, commitment evaporates; people have no tolerance for disingenuous discussions. We see this behavior from leaders so frequently that when we point it out to them, they are often puzzled by the simple idea of clearly and directly spelling out their desires. It seems that leaders have a preconceived notion that if they told their teams what they want, it would somehow disempower them.

Ironically, leaders who are *brilliant communicators* can also erode commitment. Employees may perceive a leader's language as too slick to be believed and as undermining sincerity and care. The more polished or packaged the message is, the less believable it will be. Instead of engaging employees, the leader will be seen as trying to sell his message. (See Figure 5-2 for more examples of how certain leadership traits may diminish employee commitment.)

Cold Cruel World: Commitment from Key Outsiders

The final aspect of leading from the front is to examine how wide the scope of leadership could and should be. There are other stakeholders, other people with valuable information, and other sources of support and fuel for the content of the strategy and for spreading the context of the strategy. Two examples are customers and community.

Customers are critical. Leadership across different industries can easily demonstrate inclusion of customers who will greatly assist in the eventual implementation of strategy:

- Apple is rather famous for listening to customers' comments on interface design, flexibility, recombinations of features, and so forth. The iPhone has revolutionized its market through its responsiveness to web browsing, e-mail, instant messaging, phone use, music downloads, and photo sharing.

- High-end cars such as the Mercedes SLR McLaren are offering varying seat sizes so that drivers and passengers don't have to squirm in universal seats that do not fit body extremes, no matter how many adjustments are provided. And for the rest of us who don't own a McLaren, dual controls for drivers and passengers in minivans allow husbands and wives to travel comfortably without having to engage in "It's too hot," "No, it's too cold" contests.

- Newspapers have implemented "zoning" so that foreign language sections can be delivered only to ethnic enclaves,

Commonly Regarded Leadership Traits	How They Erode Employee Commitment to a Strategy	How They Could Increase Commitment
Great Vision	Leader feels he must define the strategy and thus excludes others from it; employees feel it is "his"–not "our"–strategy.	Leader understands that his job is to get others to create the strategy with him, therefore building and sharing ownership throughout the process.
Supreme Confidence	Leader is convinced that he is right and that every aspect of the strategy is correct; employees feel he isn't open to feedback or criticism, resulting in cynicism and resignation.	Leader understands that he must set the example for openness and humility by being vulnerable, listening genuinely, and encouraging others to contribute.
Brilliant Communications	Leader believes eloquence and polish are essential for winning over employees; employees see polish as a veneer masking a strategy they won't like, resulting in skepticism and suspicion.	Leader understands that authentic communication, including admitting mistakes and not having all the answers, is more important than slick presentations.

Figure 5-2. How some leadership traits diminish employee commitment.

with more national news for some, more local news for others. Advertisers are thus able to very finely direct their promotions to highly targeted markets.

◻ A new elitism is being created by "platinum clubs" offering special accommodations on cruise ships, rental-car special services, even private eating areas in restaurants (the "chef's table" in the kitchen itself). These services have been generated by customers' requests to get away from the hum-drum and the everyday crowds in an age when anyone can buy an airline club membership and upgrading to first-class is a routine occurrence. One of the most profound examples is the "private clients" groups at banks, created for the high-asset individuals. We doubt that any enlightened bank executive would overlook listening to this group when creating the content and context necessary for commitment. For the less affluent, retailers are bringing back lay-away plans for credit-strapped customers in the post-crash world.

◻ Recreation and tourism are segments of the economy that listen closely to guests and visitors. While Disney has suffered from the impact of the current economic crisis with everyone else, it is well known for listening closely to customer needs and desires. The rides, experiences, amenities, and overall environment are areas where leadership seeks out customer input even more than employee input.

A second "outside" area to which to extend leadership is the community. Most arts groups must look to the community for support (not just financial, but allowances for parking, advertising, and special events). Consequently, they need to be seen as leaders who will improve the community not only through artistic contribution, but also through being good citizens. Curt Columbus, the artistic director of Trinity Repertory Theater, a Tony Award-winning theater in Providence, Rhode Island, refers to "the public square" as his bailiwick, and he doesn't believe that theater or its contributions begin at the front door or at the start of a performance.

StratComment

When you examine your business and organizations to determine the true scope of leadership action, don't stop at the inside of the four walls you are staring at.

Local interest groups can be vital to include in leadership. When strategy calls for relocation, expansion, reduction, inconvenience, and controversy, it is vital for the organization's leadership to be aligned with local groups. Boeing had a relatively smooth experience moving its headquarters to Chicago while leaving manufacturing in Seattle. But many leading paint manufacturers, such as Sherwin-Williams, have been fiercely prosecuted for using lead-based paint in the environment, even when there was no proof that particular houses had a particular company's paint on them. The lawsuits are driven more by an irresponsible value system than hard evidence.

There is a history of "junk science" that has bankrupted innocent companies or organizations on the fringe of some catastrophe. Johns Manville, one of the largest and most highly respected companies in the United States, was forced out of business by the asbestos scares. Corning endured great damage from what most authorities now decry as junk science in the silicone breast implant litigation. Politicians routinely use "the rich," "the special interests," "the polluters," and the "profit gougers" as populist targets, despite facts or reason (or the irony of the politicians' taking money from those "special interests," being "super rich" themselves, and building "anti-green" McMansions for themselves). We contend that leadership is better than a bunker mentality any day of the week. Johnson & Johnson demonstrated such leadership with the Tylenol tampering scare. Exxon demonstrated the reverse with the *Exxon Valdez* oil spill crisis.

Being seen as a community force and leader can help to mitigate such charges. You have to lead from the front. The advantage of being up on that horse today is that no one is shooting at you (at least not with lethal intent).

Let's now turn our attention to how this leadership produces better strategy.

CHAPTER 6

◆ ◆ ◆

TAKING A STAND–THE KEY TO STRATEGIC COMMITMENT

Why the Aztecs Put a Stake in the Ground

On May 25, 1961, U.S. President John F. Kennedy articulated a bold challenge for the country: Send a man to the moon by the end of the decade. Some thought he had lost it; others thought he was just making another move in the Cold War competition between the United States and the Soviets. He said: "I believe that this nation should commit itself to achieving the goal, before this decade is out, of landing a man on the moon and returning him safely to the Earth."

The Soviet Union had opened the space race in 1957 when it sent Sputnik into orbit. Cosmonaut Yuri Gagarin became the first man in space four years later; the Soviets were clearly beating the Americans to the final frontier.

Feeling a sense of urgency to overtake the Soviets, Kennedy huddled with Vice President Lyndon Johnson and his science advisers to come up with a plan. The president determined that the man-on-the-moon challenge would be technologically daunting, but it was a goal that the United States could reach before the Soviet Union.

Putting a Stake in the Ground Means No Retreat

The Aztec warriors were expected to tether their ankles to a stake in the ground, so that they would fight in that place or die. There was no retreat. While a radical battle standard, the phrase "stake in the ground" has stayed with us for good reason. Kennedy had planted his stake.

"No single space project in this period will be more impressive to mankind, or more important for the long-range exploration of space; and none will be so difficult or expensive to accomplish," Kennedy said. Congress took the challenge, even with Kennedy cautioning them that the cost would be significant, more than $9 billion in 1960s dollars.

Kennedy's vision to get to the moon guided every move of NASA's human space flight program. Mercury, Gemini and Apollo missions were designed with his objective in mind. Kennedy's dream became a reality on July 20, 1969, when Apollo 11 commander Neil Armstrong took a small step for himself and a "giant leap for mankind," leaving a dusty trail of footprints on the moon.

A dozen astronauts would reach the moon over the next three years, collecting rocks, driving around on a "moon buggy," and even hitting some golf balls. The Soviets scrapped their lunar program without ever landing a man on the moon. Those original astronauts have been the only humans from any country to reach the surface of the moon; even the U.S. has not tried to duplicate the feat.

StratComment

People will commit to leaders who dramatically manifest that the stake is in the ground, and they do not intend to retreat.

Late in 2003, the executive team at Capital One recognized the urgent need for a complete overhaul of their credit card billing infrastructure. Having amassed an account portfolio in excess of 40 million customers while growing rapidly over the previous ten years, the company's legacy systems were being pushed to the limit and made account customization, cross-selling, and product innovation extremely onerous tasks. Several attempts had been made over the previous three years to fix some of the pieces, but now was the time to build a system that would allow for continued growth and support the company's strategy to expand into the retail bank world. Rob Alexander, who had been head of Capital One's Credit Card business, was asked to lead the effort.

The project was enormous (eventually involving about 1,400 internal Capital One IT, marketing and operations personnel, with an additional 600-plus technology consultants), the budget big (one of the largest undertaken in the company's history) and the goals ambitious. "A major IT consulting firm assessed the project and gave us a 1% chance of meeting our target delivery date. I knew this would require extraordinary levels of commitment on behalf of everyone involved," Alexander said.

An initial core team of 30 managers, some of whom were "drafted" onto the project, was less than enthusiastic about being part of the project team. At the time the company had a spotty track record with delivering large, complex projects according to plan. There were enough examples of failed projects to raise significant concerns in people's minds as to their ability to succeed on this one, which was by far the biggest they had ever attempted. "To begin to gain their commitment, I knew we had to build a vivid and compelling vision of the future system capabilities. We settled on a simple, but enormously energizing phrase—'building the infrastructure to power innovation'—that became a galvanizing theme for everything we did," said Alexander.

After "we are trying to climb a huge mountain" became a recurring expression in management team meetings, Alexander endorsed the idea of bringing a veteran of three Everest expeditions who had himself reached the summit, to address the entire project team at the kick-off of the delivery phase of the program. The vivid descriptions of teamwork, dedication, attention to detail, and uncertainty of success involved in climbing the world's tallest mountain gave the group a life-or-death perspective on what would be required of them to succeed.

To monitor team commitment, Alexander and his leadership team conducted quarterly pulse surveys measuring team members' confidence in meeting deadlines, willingness to stay on the project, ability to raise and address tough issues, and other critical matters. The survey helped the team keep things on track. About a year into the effort, Alexander and his management team decided to switch vendors for the billing infrastructure, requiring the team to re-plan their entire approach. The pulse survey indicated even greater levels of confidence in project leadership based upon their willingness and courage to make such a difficult decision. In 2006, within budget and ahead of the original schedule, the system went live and almost immediately the benefits began to roll in. Bringing a new product to market now takes weeks, not months. Actions taken on an account by a customer service associate are automatically captured. And system maintenance costs have fallen significantly.

People Are Not "Goaled," They're Committed

Let's return for a moment to Edison Peres, vice president of distribution development and management at Lucent/Avaya, who was aiming to significantly increase the performance of his group. A good year would have meant a 20 percent increase in sales to resellers; that didn't satisfy Peres. His goal was to dramatically increase sales of products through "indirect" channels to more than $1.5 billion within three years. Many within the company, including his own sales force, did not embrace this more than tenfold increase.

"In the first couple of months, people were fighting it rather than making it happen," says Peres. "They were telling me the plan was unreasonable, if not impossible."

Thus, he didn't secure the commitment of the necessary parties to his ambitious plan right away. Through sessions focused on context issues, Peres found that most employees regarded 10 percent to 20 percent annual growth as commendable, but not Peres's goal of 100 percent. "Most of our salespeople said, 'What do you mean you're increasing my quota 100 percent? How unreasonable is that?'"

During the course of numerous meetings over several months, Peres was able to get people to fully embrace his vision and plan. In fact, they adopted the mantra of being "an unstoppable team" as one of their core commitment principles. This became a platform for addressing, head on, every obstacle that came their way.

Three years later, the initiative was a huge success. Annual revenue through indirect channels had topped $1.7 billion, while infrastructure costs increased by only a factor of four. Says Peres today: "I attribute our ability to succeed to the culture of unstoppable commitment we developed."

These stories are prime examples of executives who put their reputations and careers on the line for bold, audacious outcomes that history indicated were highly unlikely—if not impossible—to achieve. These executives had the courage to stand up (and stake out their ground) for something they believed in, despite the fact they had little supporting evidence for the certainty of its achievement. Taking a stand is a critical aspect of generating strategic commitment; it requires the type of courage that goes well beyond being open to honest and direct feedback—which in itself is not insignificant. It means staking oneself to a mission, an outcome, an ambitious future that causes one to think, act, and behave differently, and thereby inspires and enables others to do the same.

StratComment

There are countless examples of leaders helping people overcome what seemed like insurmountable odds or overwhelming opinion to the contrary, by taking a stand and then standing their ground.

We find the essence of taking a stand best captured in this quote from W. H. Murray:

Until one is committed, there is hesitancy, the chance to draw back, always ineffectiveness. Concerning all acts of initiative (and creation), there is one elementary truth, the ignorance of which kills countless ideas and splendid plans: that the moment one definitely commits oneself, then Providence moves too. All sorts of things occur to help one that would never otherwise have occurred. A whole stream of events issues from the decision, raising in one's favor all manner of unforeseen incidents and meetings and material assistance which no man could have dreamt would have come his way. I have learned a deep respect for one of Goethe's couplets: Whatever you can do or dream you can, begin it. Boldness has genius, power, and magic in it. Begin it now.

Murray was deputy leader of the 1951 Everest reconnaissance expedition. Although they did not succeed in reaching the summit, his group contributed significantly to finding the route used in 1953 by Edmund Hillary and Tenzing Norgay. The oft-quoted passage cited above appears in his 1951 book *The Scottish Himalayan Expedition*.

When the Going Gets Tough, You're Finally Making Progress

Organizations either have great results that provide great stories, or merely great stories about why they don't have great results.

In our combined consulting experience, we have found that the vast majority of organizational dysfunctionality and ineffectiveness is due to the lack of an unequivocal stand on the part of the leader, which is often due to a lack of sufficient courage.

When asked, poor leaders will provide lists of reasons that attempt to assign cause for their organizational malaise outside themselves. The reasons may include limits on authority, market conditions, regulatory constraints, or other exogenous factors and circumstances.

Time and again we see leaders initially resist the notion that their level of courage is suspect; but when these same leaders dig deeper into the source of their equivocation, they recognize that taking a stand is a risky proposition, and assigning cause to the circumstances is a safer bet. Politicians, of course, do this as a matter of habit and survival.

We begin every client engagement by conducting interviews with the executives, managers, and employees of the organization where we ask them to share their views about what is working and what is not working in their organization; we always want to know what is working but delve deeper into the areas that are preventing, hindering, or slowing progress. And, in every engagement that we have been involved in, we have found a similar pattern: The executives, managers, and employees really know what is going on. They know what the issues are, what is not working, where communication, trust, cohesion, alignment, and communication are weak or missing—and they have a good sense as to why. There is a sequence of questions that we always ask, and we almost always get the same answers.

We first ask, "How long have these dysfunctional dynamics been going on?" The common reply is "for a while" or "for many months or years" (dysfunctional dynamics have usually been around for a long time). We then ask: "Have you ever brought it up in the team?" or "Have you ever demanded that this matter get addressed?" or "Have you ever given that negative feedback to that person bluntly?" And for the most part, people admit that they haven't addressed the issue or haven't been willing to do what is needed to address the issue. And while we fully understand organizational complexities, challenges and risks, it most often boils down to courage.

> **StratComment**
>
> *People often wait for the right circumstances to be courageous. But being courageous is not the absence of fear; it is being afraid and still acting in accordance with one's stand and commitment.*

To be clear, we are not oblivious to or flippant about organizational politics and what it takes to muster the courage to make change. On the other hand, we have found that hesitancy, indecisiveness, and ineffectiveness (which are usually accompanied by excuses, stories, and justifications) are most often derived from a lack of a stand. Rather than staking out a position, too many leaders are busy looking for a path to beat a retreat, "just in case."

When open, honest, and effective communication is lacking, people often justify it with reasons such as "I didn't know what to tell them or how to say it," or "I am not a good communicator." The real issue is a lack of courage. With sufficient courage, people would insist on obtaining whatever information or expertise they felt was missing. With sufficient courage, people would not tolerate a lack of straight talk, or repeated misunderstandings, or an environment of protection and conservatism (otherwise known as CYA).

George Bernard Shaw put this very eloquently when, in *Mrs. Warren's Profession*, Act II, he wrote: "People are always blaming their circumstances for what they are. I don't believe in circumstances. The people who get on in this world are the people who get up and look for the circumstances they want, and if they can't find them, make them."

The leaders of any organization must choose if they want to generate a bold future for their organization that is based in their vision and commitment—what we call a future by design—or let the inertia of their history determine their fate—we call that a future by default. Recall Alan Kay, the former Apple Fellow who said, *"The only way to predict the future is to invent it."* In order to take on a future that is greater than its historical limitations, an organization, starting with its leaders, must take a stand.

When leaders take a stand about the future of their organization they are raising the bar and deliberately elevating their relationship with their future, each other, their managers and employees, as well as with themselves. Taking a stand is not a guarantee, but it *is* a promise from leaders to strengthen their courage, resolve, sincerity, and caring. It is a promise to dedicate the time, effort, and commitment necessary to become the type of leaders who can live up to and drive the bold vision of their organization. It is about staking themselves to their desired future so that (taking a page from the Aztecs or even Sun Tzu*) there is no retreat. It includes an implicit and explicit promise to generate an environment of strategic commitment, such that everyone feels genuinely and passionately committed and accountable for that shared future.

To repeat Murray's words, "The moment one definitely commits oneself, then Providence moves too." We have witnessed this time and time again.

When President Kennedy declared that the United States should commit to sending a man to the moon, it was an unrealistic commitment because none of the key technologies required to achieve such a daunting mission—food, fuel, materials—existed. His persistence set in motion, however, a whole stream of events that, while not always flowing smoothly, eventually led to the desired outcome.

When Gandhi took on the cause of a free India, at first no one paid attention to him or took him seriously because he was one man, without power, authority, or status, and the vision he was proclaiming seemed to be daunting and unrealistic. But he moved from stereotypical London lawyer to charismatic nonviolent leader of millions.

Lee Iacocca saved Chrysler during his stint as CEO by staking out positions on loans, unions, new products (convertibles and minivans), and personal assurances. Mercedes-Benz had a disaster on its hands when it bought Chrysler, because it was disingenuous about its motives (it was an acquisition, not the publicly proclaimed "merger of equals") and no one could find a stake in the ground anywhere.

---

* Sun Tzu pointed out that soldiers fought better if you made them smash their rice pots, because then commitment to winning the battle was the only way to ensure they would eat. Likewise, various Asian generals made their men burn the boats that brought them to new shores. Many of us in management are probably unwilling to smash our own rice pots—and we pay the price every day with less-than-stellar results.

As noted, Gordon Bethune, as CEO of Continental Airlines, said that the company would be first or second in the industry in baggage delivery accuracy, on-time arrivals, and fewest customer complaints. And he said that if these goals were accomplished, every employee would share in a bonus. When they missed one year because of what he thought was a statistical error, he awarded the bonus anyway.

Taking a stand may seem to imply committing once and being forever locked in, without room for flexibility or adjustments. What a rigid notion; as we have seen firsthand many times, taking a stand is quite the opposite. It requires leaders to lead their organizations with two seemingly contradictory perspectives simultaneously: complete resolve and rigidity alongside flexibility and creativity. On one hand, it means staying relentlessly focused and committed to their vision and future state and, on the other, continuing to stay open-minded about the strategies, routes, and means to get there, without hesitation—to take risks at times in order to explore ways that were not originally contemplated.

In so many organizations, even when a great strategy has been established, people's relationship with it is weak. If it is simple enough they'll hang a declaration of the company strategy in their cubicle, and if it is more complex, they'll have it on their computer in a PowerPoint presentation only to be used once or twice a year when they have to give a talk. Their daily actions, behaviors, attitudes, and priorities are not shaped and determined by the strategy, however. When the leaders have taken a stand for a bold and compelling future for their organization, they have in essence constituted themselves as that future, just as Gandhi did when he constituted himself as his commitment for a "free India;" as Martin Luther King did with respect to equal rights for African-Americans; Steve Jobs did with his company's "insanely great products."

In other words, if vast, philosophic, geopolitical ideas can be instantiated through firmness of leadership, it is not unreasonable to expect that organizational aspirations—whether product commercialization, more dramatic customer service, investment strategies, or new market initiatives—can be similarly embodied by enlightened leaders.

Success and Failure Ebb and Flow, but Courage Cannot

When Mark Adams (all names in this example are fictionalized), vice president of APAC distribution for an international high-tech company, moved his family from California to Singapore in the winter of 2006, he knew he had his work cut out for him. In his new role he was charged with improving service speed and quality. The regional team he inherited was really struggling. His managers, who were in their positions for a long time, had lost their passion, energy, courage, and commitment regarding their role and the value they could provide.

His overall team had gotten so used to relating to itself as a back office, operational, transactional, and tactical function that its entire orientation, mind-set, and outlook about its potential impact and value were quite small. The team, even its leaders, had a "followers" mentality. They were constantly reacting to headquarters' requests, tasks, and fire drills, but rarely initiating, leading, driving, impacting, and providing real strategic value.

The dynamic of low self-image and esteem, low performance and value, and low reputation was on a downward spiral, and Adams was determined to turn things around. "The fact that Mark was an American ex-pat did not help. As a matter of fact, in the beginning people were very skeptical about his prospects to succeed," says Grant Tucker, who is one of his senior leaders and confidants. Everyone knew the team wasn't functioning well and they expected Adams to make personnel changes immediately, but instead he took a different route with a bolder stand. He invited all the senior leaders, including those who reported to him and those who reported to the country leaders (who at that time did not have a high degree of respect for

Adams's organization) and their direct reports—the top thirty-five leaders—to a three-day vision and commitment session.

"In that session, we confronted our reality very bluntly, especially the places where we were not functioning as a team and not acting with courage. It became very clear to all of us that instead of behaving like victims of the circumstances we could take on a much bolder and more effective game, which we all wanted to do," shares Colleen Forster, distribution leader in New Zealand. In that initial session the leaders crafted a vision for their future, as well as specific strategic promises they were determined to fulfill. They all left the session having taken a stand and committing to a new level of collaboration and determination to provide greater value to their region.

"The following months included a lot of hard work and change, including changing many of the players who were not up to the new game," admits Adams. "But we were determined to elevate our impact and status in order to succeed." In the last operational review in 2008 Adams's boss, Drew Moran, senior vice president of worldwide distribution, concluded the intense six-hour session by acknowledging Adams and his leaders for the remarkable transformation that they had been able to bring about in APAC in the last year, including providing significant value and elevating the status and reputation of distribution. "I acknowledge you for putting distribution on the map in APAC," were Moran's closing words.

"This says it all," says Monica Woods, Moran's HR leader. "It was very clear in the performance review that Mark's bold vision and strategic promises were becoming a reality."

People are committed, not "goaled." It is a commitment to behave a certain way rather than to merely pursue a set of objectives. Counterintuitively, perhaps, *the bolder the objectives, the more they will demand a new order of mind-set and behaviors.*

As mentioned previously, Edison Peres's team committed to being an "unstoppable team" in order to reach new levels of thinking and action. What that meant for them was that they would be unwilling to allow circumstances and conditions to be insurmountable. While the team understood that this was not a guarantee that they would, in fact, be able to overcome every barrier and obstacle that came their way, their declaration forced them to adopt a very different attitude. On a regular basis, they challenged each other to be "un-circumstantial" and "unconditional" (as they referred to it) in their commitments. They became more self-aware of the way they communicated.

Phrases such as "we can't do that" or "that is not possible" were not accepted, and when faced with challenges that seemed unsolvable they often held brainstorming sessions where the only rule was that the meeting would not end until they had found a viable way to proceed. "There were many things that came our way that were out of our control" said Peres's operations director. "However, we knew we had 100 percent control over our relationship with all of that. We knew that we couldn't choose the circumstances, but we *could* choose how to respond to them."

"Making the numbers did not only mean achieving the $1.7 billion. It meant making every month's numbers without missing the forecast and commitment" says Edison. "Prior to committing we didn't deliver our monthly plan consistently. However, with the change in our focus and attitude not only did we start delivering every month, but we became *the* go-to organization for making up the numbers when other organizations failed to deliver. We became one of *the* most reliable and counted on teams from a delivery standpoint" Edison continues.

This is an absolute bedrock point for our approach to strategic commitment: *It's not so much what happens, but it's what you then do about it.* Committed teams see just another challenge to overcome, even in adverse conditions.

Once leaders take a stand, they must get the rest of their managers and employees to do the same. This unfolds as follows:

- The hallway conversations begin to change as more and more people get on board. In the absence of the organization taking a deliberate stand, the watercooler conversations are more apathetic, cynical, resistant, and skeptical. As the leaders step up, people move toward compliance, curiosity, and ultimately ownership, commitment, and accountability (see Figure 6-1).

- The more people take a stand for the future of the organization, the more you will have an environment of strategic commitment.

- It is unrealistic to expect 100 percent of the organization to be at the highest rung of the ladder 100 percent of the time. There will always be a spread. The CEO's job is to continue to move people up the ladder, from apathy to showing curiosity to being fully committed to the desired future. Obviously, the further up this ladder people are, the more owners and partners the CEO will have in pursuing organizational objectives. This is not about reaching perfection; it's about continuing to drive progress.

- To generate an environment of strategic commitment, the CEO and others in leadership must create an environment in which people are coached, encouraged, and invited, and demanded to move up the ladder. Their job is to continue to communicate about, and enroll people in, the possibility represented by the new future, and the critical role everyone can play in realizing it.

Dedication for Him Isn't Necessarily So for Her: Tailoring Commitment

CEOs need to be prepared for the cynicism and resistance they will encounter when attempting to introduce significant change. The

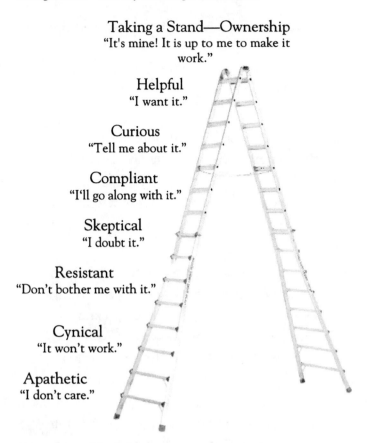

Taking a Stand—Ownership
"It's mine! It is up to me to make it work."

Helpful
"I want it."

Curious
"Tell me about it."

Compliant
"I'll go along with it."

Skeptical
"I doubt it."

Resistant
"Don't bother me with it."

Cynical
"It won't work."

Apathetic
"I don't care."

Figure 6-1. The ladder of strategic commitment.

bigger the stand they take, the greater the cynicism. It's like an image of a mountain reflecting in the waters of the lake. The higher the mountain, the bigger its reflection is in the lake. We have found that there are two types of leaders when it comes to change—those who take the biggest stand they can, knowing it will generate high levels of cynicism, and those who try to reduce or avoid dealing with the cynicism, hence reducing their stands to the smallest position they can take.

George Bernard Shaw also said in *Man and Superman* that there are two types of people: "The reasonable man adapts himself to the world; the unreasonable one who persists in trying to adapt the world to himself. Therefore, all progress depends on the unreason-able man."

The leader's road is often a tough one, but a critical one to establish and travel. Here is some advice:

- Taking a stand doesn't mean that things will progress smoothly. On the contrary, often it is the opposite. When leaders take a stand they are deliberately bringing up and inviting the challenges, issues, gaps, and dysfunctions that were previously under the carpet so that these matters can be addressed.

- After taking a stand, leaders often feel that things have gotten worse rather than better. "This is not because things have actually deteriorated since you've taken a stand," we tell them. "It's just that you are more attuned to what is going on; you can see better!" Part of the courage that is required from leaders when taking a stand is to be willing to tolerate the fact that things will get worse (or seem worse) before they get better; the numbers may go down before going up. This is the Achilles heel of many leaders. They can't tolerate things getting worse so they continue to play the same game at the same level. They won't rock the boat. (One of the tough things about the fog lifting is that you see what the fog was hiding.)

- When leaders take bolder stands they commit to bigger objectives and deliverables, and it is inevitable that eventually ("sooner or sooner," as we like to say) they'll have setbacks in their commitment. They'll promise ten and deliver three or even less. But that's better than promising two and delivering two, or not promising anything at all.

- When there are failures in delivery, leaders will have two ways to approach it. One way takes you backward, while the other helps move things toward the desired future, strengthens the organization, and increases the likelihood of future successes.

The common, mindless, automatic reaction to failure in delivery is to look for fault and blame. Leaders often get quite upset when expectations are not met in areas that are considered important to them (or in areas that they are being expected to deliver on by their superiors). What happens next is that, out of frustration or anger, an investigation committee launches a witch hunt! "Whose fault is it?" Executives, managers, and employees who have been around for a while are so used to seeing this happen that they immediately go into their survival mode. It's an automatic reflex. When leadership is looking to assign blame, everyone will be busy hiding, covering, deferring, misrepresenting, and lying. This goes on in organizations every day, and it completely undermines any potential for learning from failures and mistakes. When the hallway conversation is geared toward avoiding blame, no one will take the risk of participating in, contributing to, or providing insight into what really went wrong. Even those who are close to the situation will be very reluctant to give away information; "We find ourselves being economical with the truth" is the way one executive describes these situations. This common dynamic ensures that the same mistakes will repeat themselves.

> **StratComment**
>
> *Commitment can only be achieved when the hunt is for cause and not for blame. This extends from the board right down to the frontline.*

In high-performing environments, the dynamic is radically different. When things go wrong, which they inevitably will, the CEO will get the leadership team together and make it clear that he is not looking for blame and he does not care about whose fault it is. Rather, the CEO will take advantage of the opportunity to engage all the relevant stakeholders who are involved in the situation in an open, honest, and effective conversation and ask, "What happened?" "What was missing?" "What was in the way?" "What can we learn from this?" and "What needs to be corrected?" When people feel assured that no one cares about fault, they will be very inclined to work together to figure out how to ensure the same mistakes never happen again.

Jim Burns's U.K. management team asked him to relinquish his intense control and involvement in managing the weekly revenue commitments and instead empower them to fully own and manage the ongoing performance of their billion-dollar telecom business. And so he did. Even as the end of the quarter was coming close and it was getting clearer that the numbers were at risk, he continued to stay away while providing support from a distance.

"This was not easy for me to do," says Burns. "We are the second largest operation in our company and the largest in Europe, and the company depends on us." The unit missed that quarter and, to add insult to injury, their gap was bigger than they had anticipated, so in addition to not meeting their numbers their gap was surprisingly bigger than their prediction.

"Everyone was afraid of Jim's reaction," says Peter McNally, Burns's HR leader. "We were all expecting him to come down on us pretty badly. Plus, people were mostly concerned that this failure would cause him to not trust us, change his mind, and step right back in to control the weekly performance."

But Burns did not do that. He gathered his senior team for an urgent meeting in which he expressed his disappointment, but then, instead of focusing on blame or fault, he engaged the team in a dialogue about how to ensure this would never happen again. "The quarter was over and there was nothing we could do at that point to change our disappointing results," said Burns. "So all that was left was to ensure that we really learned from this experience so that we could elevate the game from this point on. I wanted my leaders to step up, so rather than making them feel bad, I requested them to elevate their game, and they seemed quite enthusiastic about that."

The meeting was very productive, and as a result the team fully owned up to the fact that they were not on top of their game. They also came up with several initiatives to cause change, one of which was to reinvent their forecasting process, especially its timeliness and accuracy. "There are only two things you can do with your past failures," says Burns. "Either use them to elevate your game or use them to justify why you can't do better. There was only one option for us, and I have already seen a significant improvement in the responsibility and performance of my team since that last quarter."

The following quarter was a challenging one, given the economic reality in Europe and the United Kingdom. However, the U.K. team was able to achieve great results—and everyone seemed to agree that it was a significant achievement that looked doubtful throughout the last half of 2008.

If you listen to the hallway or watercooler conversations in organizations that are high-performing and then eavesdrop on organizations that are ineffective, you'll notice they have quite a different flavor. High-performers are oriented around creating, inventing, causing, and delivering bold *results*, while ineffective organizations are full of reporting, tracking, monitoring, and explaining *activities*.

When things go wrong, the contrast is amplified. In ineffective organizations, conversations are oriented around stories, reasons, explanations, excuses, and justifications for why things are not happening or did not happen. "Because of . . ." "They didn't come through with . . . "If only X had happened . . ." "They should have done Y . . ." These types of remarks are pervasive, and they are all designed to place the cause for weak performance outside of anyone's responsibility.

In contrast, conversations in high-performing organizations are oriented around solving, improving, correcting, and learning so that errors are not repeated. "How can we fix this?" "What can we learn from this?" "What can we do to ensure this does not happen again?" There is no witch hunt, since that would only, inevitably instill fear and CYA behaviors down the road.

There will always be mistakes, setbacks, and breakdowns on the road to strategic commitment—those are inevitable. Powerful leaders use setbacks as opportunities, not in a Pollyanna way, but authentically, to identify what went wrong, to revisit and solidify their commitment to success, and to grow the organizational capability to deal with these kinds of issues. Conversely, ineffective leaders assign cause to factors beyond anyone's control, find someone or something to blame (often finding a fall guy who was unlucky enough to be absent from that one meeting), and create an environment in which no one will take ownership for anything for fear of being tarred with a career-limiting or career-ending failure.

Leaders need to take a stand that is specific enough so that everyone is on the same page, marching to the same drummer in the same direction, while remaining flexible enough to give different people room to participate and express their commitment in their own unique ways.

You see, the Aztec stake in the ground had one significant drawback: It was tough to take the initiative and march forward. Let's look now at another key ingredient for leading the change.

♦ ♦ ♦

CHAPTER 7

BUILDING AND RESTORING TRUST

Essential Competencies for Generating Strategic Commitment

While current business and management literature extols the virtues of building organizational cultures based on speed, empowerment, customer intimacy, and trust, it seems the most critical of these is perhaps the least accessible. Without *trust*, speed produces rework, empowerment is regarded as a buzzword that generates more cynicism than effective action, and customers find others who will consistently deliver on promises.

But while much has been written about the *need* for, and *benefits* of, a trusting environment, the advice on what must be done to *build* trust is sparse. To do so, individuals and teams must be able to first identify, and then build upon, the levels of trust within their work environment. These competencies are fundamental to achieving dramatic improvements in ownership, communication, and performance associated with an environment of strategic commitment.

What Is Trust, Anyway?

As a starting point, we must recognize that trust, like beauty, means different things to different people. For example, someone might say, "I don't trust her because she's never on time." And yet someone else might say of that same punctuality-challenged individual, "I trust her completely—she always makes quota." In another instance, a lack of trust might be attributed not to any specific behavior, but to a kind of gut feeling: "I can't put my finger on it, but there's something about the guy that makes me suspicious."

This less-grounded assessment of trust, while not uncommon and not necessarily invalid, makes the building of trust a decidedly elusive undertaking. Further complicating the issue are situations wherein our trust of another is based on third-party opinions, the validity of which may be suspect.

If the intent is to build an environment where one can authentically say of their leaders and coworkers "I trust them," and the coworkers and leaders can say the same in turn, we must first establish a common understanding of what is meant by the term.

A Working Definition

We propose that trust is a function of four distinct behavioral characteristics that together form the criteria for its assessment. These are:

- Being Honest
- Being Dependable
- Exercising Judgment
- Generating Partnership

Being able to fully trust another (whether or not that trust is ever verbalized) is a function of being genuinely satisfied with each of these criteria. To whatever degree trust is lacking, the source of the gap can always be traced to one or more of the four dimensions described in more detail below.

StratComment

Four characteristics aren't too much to ask for, but are we asking for them at all?

These four characteristics of trust also link directly to the four context drivers of strategic commitment (see Figure 7-1). Being honest and authentic directly supports people's assessment of their leader's credibility and sincerity. Demonstrating courage and resolve means that one acts dependably in the face of fear, discomfort, or difficult circumstances. Real competency is demonstrated by exercising sound judgment; otherwise it is merely knowledge, not competence. And care and concern are evidenced by the degree to which people are able to build partnerships across functions, levels, and geographies.

Being Honest (Authenticity, Forthrightness, Veracity, Sincerity)

By being honest, we mean two things: being forthright and being authentic. Being *forthright* is telling the plain and simple truth, without deception or distortion. If you ask, "Were you at the 2:00 p.m. budget meeting yesterday?" trust will quickly be destroyed if the answer does not match what actually took place. If someone says they will endorse your capital spending proposal and then fails to do so, trust is broken. We are making a distinction here between speaking honestly and "saying everything on your mind."

An honest answer may sometimes be: "I'm not comfortable discussing that at work," or "I will have to check with Juanita before I give you that information," or "I don't think it's appropriate for me to tell you my opinion of the new system until we are all discussing it in the meeting tomorrow." Being honest, but discriminating, builds trust by creating safety.

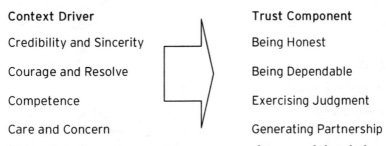

Context Driver	Trust Component
Credibility and Sincerity	Being Honest
Courage and Resolve	Being Dependable
Competence	Exercising Judgment
Care and Concern	Generating Partnership

Figure 7-1. Strategic commitment context drivers and their link to trust.

Being *authentic* means being clear and transparent about what is driving your behavior, your decisions and actions, and the intentions you are advancing. Someone can be honest in the sense of accurately reporting facts and events, but what is driving him to report on those specific events? If, for example, one team member states that another member's performance has declined three months running, the accuracy of the statement is readily determined. What is not as obvious is the agenda he is advancing by making the statement. If he is speaking in support of being a high-performing, all-for-one-and-one-for-all team, trust expands. If he is attempting to subvert the credibility of another and advance his own position, trust deteriorates.

Authenticity also includes the dimension of believing that people *mean* what they are saying, specifically regarding their intent to fulfill the promises they are making. With organizational politics alive and well within most companies, distrust as a function of perceived deception is a common and quite destructive phenomenon.

Illustration. The launch of a new regional brand was under consideration by one of the world's largest brewers. The managing director and heads of sales and marketing were debating the pros and cons of which department should own the launch. Each department, in turn, made its case for ownership of the launch, presenting accurate and relevant data in support of its position (no one disputed the data). However, as the presentations were being made, everyone involved knew that the real agenda behind each manager's passion was the belief that the predicted success of the new product would make them look good and enhance their career.

All of the talk about "What's best for the company?" had little to do with the discussion. Once these concealed agendas were divulged a far more productive conversation occurred, resulting in a decision to share ownership for elements of the launch most appropriate to the respective manager's strengths and capabilities.

Being Dependable (Reliability, Consistency, Follow-through)

By being *dependable*, we mean several things. Does the person consistently deliver on her commitments? Does she reliably manage her time, resources, and those around her in a manner that allows her to meet her commitments? Does she report back about commitments she makes without being reminded? Or is she full of excuses, reasons, rationalizations, and justifications for slipped deadlines and results that fall short, time after time?

No one meets all of their commitments 100 percent of the time; mistakes happen, balls get dropped, priorities change. But trust is built when people consistently fulfill commitments while managing the unexpected in ways that allow them to be assessed as dependable, reliable, and consistent. For example, finding out at 8:30 a.m. Monday morning that the person who promised you information for your 9:00 a.m. meeting now cannot deliver produces a lack of trust in this person's future promises. If, on the other hand, he had informed you of his inability to deliver by the previous Wednesday, other arrangements could have been made.

Effective promise management leads to an increased level of trust, whereas consistently revoked, delayed, or unfulfilled promises inevitably reduce the degree to which someone can be counted on. Consistency is vital as well. A manager who is perceived to favor one individual or group over another loses credibility among her team members. And the boss who says, "My door is always open, please come talk with me about any issue," and then proceeds to explode upon receiving bad news is sending two very different messages, producing uncertainty and tentativeness in her team.

Being dependable also means acting consistent with promises, even when you are uncomfortable, not in the mood, uncertain about how to fulfill those promises, or afraid to do what is needed to follow through. In every organization, there are the "go to" people who are turned to when times are challenging or when the stakes are high. They are trusted because—irrespective of their title, position, or location—they have demonstrated time and again that they will go beyond their comfort zone and do whatever is needed to deliver on their commitments.

Illustration. Mike, a senior manager within the sales division of a large telecom equipment manufacturer, is widely recognized as an expert regarding the products his company offers. He is also honest. If you ask him about specific conversations or events, he will tell the truth. But Mike repeatedly fails to deliver on commitments and fails to communicate in advance regarding those shortfalls. There's always a story and excuses about how busy and important he is. His team members regularly bump into issues and areas that Mike promised to address but left incomplete. While Mike's contribution and impact based on his product and market expertise has been exceptional, his lack of response and follow-through has made his peers increasingly frustrated, hence reducing his involvement in their projects.

Exercising Judgment (Ability, Capability, Capacity, Decision Making, Wisdom)

Is the person *able* to deliver on the promises he makes? Does the person have the wherewithal to fulfill whatever it is he is committing to? Or is he in over his head? Does the person make wise choices? While someone may be sincere about his promise to double sales within the region over the next budgeting period, lack of experience in a new market or with a new product portfolio makes it highly unlikely that it can be done. Furthermore, making commitments that stretch too far from previously demonstrated skills and abilities undermines the degree to which a person is trusted. Conversely, a healthy dose of reality about one's own abilities can help elicit support from others toward the achievement of even bold or audacious goals.

This dimension of trust can be quite situation-specific. For example, someone who makes and delivers on promises related to individual sales targets might be ill-equipped to assume the role of managing a sales team. The overall assessment of trust in another's abilities is determined by the degree to which the person makes choices, decisions, and commitments that are considered thoughtful, responsible, and appropriate to her position, level of competence, and her own representation of personal performance capabilities.

Additionally, trust can be undermined by being oblivious to the impact one's behavior has on those around him. When people are constantly remarking, "Why in the heck did he do *that?*" it is a sure sign that trust is or will soon be in question.

Illustration. Vince, a rising star as the production superintendent of a manufacturing operation, gets promoted to general manager. As the operation is preparing to commence a large capital project within a department unfamiliar to Vince, he declines offers of support from headquarters and sets out to demonstrate his leadership and management effectiveness by going it alone. Within a short period of time the project becomes mired in cost and time overruns, and Vince is clearly in trouble. His penchant for

> **StratComment**
> *True partnership is collaboration leavened with trust, wherein failure can strengthen and the benefit of the doubt is always extended.*

independence—while admirable in some instances—indicates a poor ability to self-assess and a clear lack of judgment and humility, and in this case it costs the success of the project.

Generating Partnership (Mutual Support, Shared Values and Concerns, Collaboration, Alliance Building)

Independent of any formal or legal agreements (none of which seem to have any direct bearing on trust anyhow), when we talk about *generating partnership* we mean creating relationships between individuals and groups in which all parties have a sense that their respective futures are connected. This may include a sense of looking out for the well-being and concerns of others, or demonstrating an interest in the areas that matter to others.

A more esoteric dimension, this ability to generate partnership takes trust to a much higher level than the other three components. For example, when someone feels a strong sense of partnership with another, she is much more able to forgive missed commitments and breakdowns. Dealt with from inside the context of partnership, missed commitments can in fact be opportunities to strengthen and deepen the level of trust. Instead of finding fault and assessing blame, the parties can enter a dialogue to look for a mutually beneficial solution.

The other dimension of partnership is having a sense of shared values: Will the person make choices over time that are based on commonly held values and principles, whether or not those have been made explicit? From our observations, the highest levels of trust are reached between people who operate based on commonly shared convictions, rather than finely crafted, detailed prescriptions and procedures.

Illustration. Tim is the president of a union local with more than 600 members. Don, the manager most closely linked to the local union, has been tasked with reducing overtime expenses. Both parties are aware that the potential for friction and conflict are quite high because this classic win-lose scenario has played out countless times before. In this case, however, all the ingredients for trust are in place. Both Tim and Don have dealt with each other honestly, they have been dependable regarding promises made, they respect the ability of the other to perform his duties, and they are up-front about what is driving them. Ultimately, they even share common concerns about the viability of the company that pays salaries, along with the need for a safe, motivated, and contributing workforce.

From this platform of trust, the two men are able to explore together a variety of paths to accomplish their mutual objectives. And with each productive and collaborative discussion, including dealing with the most sensitive and contentious of topics, partnership and trust expand.

The Real Question: How Is Trust Built?

One of the first steps in any building activity is surveying the territory upon which the construction is planned, and the first step is telling the truth, as we've said repeatedly. To that end, the matrix shown in Figure 7-2 can be used to assess the level of trust between individuals or teams. To use the matrix, you'll need to list the names of the person or team most critical to the success of the person filling out the form. A plus (+) sign indicates total satisfaction with the person or team in terms of the specific trust component, whereas a minus (-) indicates dissatisfaction and an equal sign (=) is neutral. (Numbers can be used to determine degrees of satisfaction or dissatisfaction, i.e., 5 is less satisfied than 10.)

This entirely subjective tool is designed to illuminate specific areas in which trust is missing between two or more parties at any given point in time, allowing the user to focus energy on addressing issues with precision and clarity. (Note: We are not referring here to terminable breakdowns in trust, such as misappropriating company funds, harassing a coworker, or other egregious offenses. In those instances, the appropriate action may well be terminating the professional relationship.) Any rating less than total satisfaction (that is, not marked with a "+") is grounds for initiating a dialogue aimed at building trust. Assessing oneself should be based on the degree to which you feel you are trusted by the other parties listed.

Taking examples from the matrix shown in Figure 7-2, it is readily apparent that conversations with Paula would be quite different from those with George. Dealing with issues of honesty and dependability (with George) are far more basic than those around deepening or expanding a sense of real partnership (with Paula).

You first need to ask yourself: "Am I willing to do what is necessary to build trust with this individual (or group)?" It is critical to recognize that you can answer "yes" to this question without knowing precisely *how* to achieve success. For myriad reasons, from resignation

Individual or Team	Being Honest	Being Dependable	Exercising Judgment	Generating Partnership
Self (the user)	+	+	=	=
Sales	+	+	=	=
Manufacturing	+	-	-	-
Finance	-	+	+	-
R & D	+	-	+	-
Paula	+	+	+	=
George	-	-	+	-
Karen	+	-	+	+
Michael	-	-	-	+

Figure 7-2. Trust assessment matrix.

about the possibility of success, cynicism regarding the other party's perceived willingness and openness, or an apparently overwhelming amount of historical baggage, initiating a conversation aimed at building trust may appear daunting to you. First comes the desire and the willingness to build trust, next comes finding a pathway to producing the desired outcome.

However, if you answered the question "no," distancing yourself from those with whom you are unwilling to restore trust may be the necessary option. Unfortunately, avoiding trust issues leads to work environments filled with resentment, frustration, rework, chronic dissatisfaction, and poor coordination, leaving people feeling defeated, cynical, and deflated. On the other hand, if a relationship is too important (or painful) to ignore, you must set out to overcome your fears, doubts, and concerns and confront the issue head on.

The "Building Trust Dialogue"

Once you make a choice to invest the time and energy in building or restoring trust, how to proceed is another matter. Being direct and telling someone "I don't trust you" can be quite taxing. If you are on the receiving end of such a statement it is even more difficult, and perhaps impossible, not to have your internal protection reflexes triggered. The "you" in "I don't trust *you*" will think of all the plus components of the matrix and become defensive. If, however, the speaker can point to the plus (+) areas of satisfaction *and* to the specific minus (-) areas of dissatisfaction, the listener is much more likely to hear and accept the feedback.

There are many possible paths to restoring trust among coworkers and team members. Going whitewater rafting or taking a survival course together can allow for great strides to be made in this area. However, our direct experience suggests breakthroughs that happen *in the workplace environment* produce a far more sustainable shift because they are immune from the "now we're back at work in the real world" disclaimer. We therefore suggest a format designed to allow individuals and teams to systematically address areas and issues wherein trust is missing, and that can be utilized in any location private conversations can occur. With the full recognition that trust building is not guaranteed by any one formula or silver bullet, this robust five-step approach outlines one proven methodology.

Five Steps to Recovering and Building Trust

Step One—Identify the Trust Issues. Use the trust assessment matrix to identify precisely which component or components of trust are lacking for the individual or team concerned. List specific events or incidents that have contributed to the lack of trust in any given area. The aim is to get clear on the trust issues *and* identify their source. For example, if we use George's ratings from Figure 7-2, specific events or conversations that led to assessing George as less than honest, dependable, and a good partner should be noted. Resist the temptation to generalize and keep things vague; being specific and rigorous will help you in later steps. Identifying specific promises missed is much more useful than saying, "George never keeps his promises."

Step Two—Set Up an Effective Dialogue. Request a conversation with the individual in question (George) for the purpose of addressing the lack of trust. Do not say, "I can't trust you." The person who shows up for that meeting is not likely to be open to exploring new ways of working together. A suggested script for the invitation might be to say, "(George), I'd like to have a conversation with you about improving how we're working together. I'd like to set aside at least an hour (more if necessary) for the conversation. Are you open to doing that?" This invitation will vary if there is a reporting relationship involved between the individuals. But the principle is the same—an explicit request to engage in a conversation for improving something, not for punishing, persecuting or inflicting pain.

Then, agree on a time to get together. It is obviously desirable to have the conversation in person so you can look each other in the eye and be more personal. However, it is often the case that people work in remote locations and it's just not workable or it will take too long until you will see each other in person. In these cases you'll need to make the call about the urgency of the conversation. If you conclude that it is critical to create a breakthrough in trust sooner rather than later, then you should have the conversation via a video conference, if you have that option, or by phone. We have witnessed many breakthroughs in trust conducted through phone-based dialogues. The point here is not to let the medium of communication determine the pace at which you address these issues.

> ### StratComment
>
> *Honesty involves being candid about shortcomings and problems, because not facing them means you do not have respect for the other party and don't wish to be helpful. Instead, you are avoiding your own discomfort.*

Step Three—Put the Issues on the Table. Don't rush into the topic at hand. Begin the face-to-face conversation by setting the stage. Begin by saying, "Thank you for being willing to have this conversation with me. Before we start, let me say what I am interested in accomplishing." State your desire to establish a new relationship, clear something up that has been an issue for a long time (or has just recently become an issue), be more in partnership, improve collaboration between your groups, and so on.

In order to clearly articulate the trust issues you are having with the other person, you can introduce the trust assessment matrix (Figure 7-2) and establish this framework as a way to view and assess the challenges that you are there to address.

Then continue the conversation in the following way: "(George), we've been working now for X months together, and I need to address some issues that I believe are preventing us from working together most effectively. One involves my perception that you misrepresented and inaccurately reported regarding XYZ project. Another issue is that in the last X months on several occasions you promised to deliver Y and did not do so." Be sure to differentiate between factual observations (i.e. "You promised to call me by the end of the day and you never called.") from your perceptions, interpretations and feelings (i.e. "You didn't call me because I'm not important to you and you don't care about my projects.") This rigor will help clarify the issues, minimize defensiveness, and help both parties be more responsible. Review the exact instances; address each component of trust in turn, acknowledging areas of satisfaction as well as dissatisfaction, letting the receiver of the feedback first understand and then respond to gain clarification and clear up any misunderstandings.

You must manage the conversation with an effective balance between being honest and not causing the other person to get defensive. Push yourself, however, to be crystal clear about where trust has been missing; do not settle for agreeing that something was simply a misunderstanding if you believe that hasn't been the case. The purpose of this step is to tell the truth about the current state of the relationship, which can only be accomplished with clear, unambiguous, and rationalization-free discussion about what has transpired to date. While the conversation should contain compassion and understanding, there is no room for vagueness or obfuscation.

You can use the questions below (some or all of them) to address other dimensions of the relationship that might be affecting the level of trust:

- Is there anything that has happened between us/our groups that makes it hard for us to work together?

- Have I/we done anything that made you distrust me/us? Have I/we ever let you down?

- Have I/we ever done anything that hurt your feelings or left you feeling disrespected?

- Is there anything else that I/we have done that might keep us from working together effectively?

- Do you feel you can be open with me/us? How can I/we make it easier for you to do that?

- What's missing for us to have the most effective partnership?

Allow the conversation to be two-way, and drive for genuine understanding and connection on each topic you raise. Then address and agree on specific actions necessary to resolve any outstanding promises or commitments. You may need to cancel some agreements, renegotiate others, and forgive or apologize as needed to have an experience where you make peace with the past.

Step three is a very critical step because in order to achieve the breakthrough you want in trust, you need to ensure that both

> **StratComment**
>
> *The extraordinary aspect of honest exchange is that it can instantly form a new beginning and shed all the old baggage and obstacles to performance.*

parties are honestly expressing their feelings and that both parties are genuinely listening and taking things to heart. When moderating such conversations, we always coach people to "open their ears and hearts to what the other party is saying." In this step, the first person should fully express his feelings about where trust is missing and then the other person should have a turn as well. While one is expressing the other should only listen, and vice versa. We always recommend that each party in turn say "Thank you" after the other has fully expressed his issues. This is in gratitude for the other's courage and commitment to the relationship (after all, if they didn't care they wouldn't have confronted the issue, especially since it is tough on both parties). This and the next two steps can also benefit from the use of a facilitator whose impartiality and competence are respected by both parties.

Step Four—Create a New Way Forward. When you express your issues and frustrations openly, honestly, and directly and the person you are expressing your issues to listens and understands, there is a release and "emptiness" that follows, a sense of "so now what?" This "clean slate" is the best place from which to rebuild trust and create a new dynamic in the relationship.

In this step, rather than rushing into actions, take the time to speculate and create a new beginning. Engage in a conversation to answer questions such as, "What could a great relationship look like?" "What are we committed to in our relationship?" "How would you envision us working together, ideally?" and "What could be possible—what could we accomplish—if we had really strong trust?" If you do this step right, you will find yourselves getting quite excited about the potential of a new level of partnership and trust.

Once you have explored what could be possible and how it will look and feel, you should move to the final step of cementing the possibility into a new way of acting and behaving.

Step Five—Align on New Behaviors and Practices. Establish whatever practices, behaviors, and routines both parties feel are supportive of maintaining, building, and cementing the space of trust and partnership you discussed in step four. The parties may agree to periodic face-to-face or telephone meetings, regular conversations to assess the level of mutual trust (possibly using the assessment matrix or any other tools), or the assistance and involvement of a mutually agreed upon third party. Overdo the support mechanisms at the beginning—they can always be reduced once trust has been restored. Figure 7-3 is a list of behaviors that increase or decrease trust. This list can be useful in support of designing specific actions required.

Finally, complete the conversation by thanking the other parties for their participation and acknowledging progress made.

Moving Forward

If done well, the five-step process for recovering and building trust between the involved parties will produce a sense of freshness, affinity, and willingness to look ahead. There will be the experience of desiring to make the partnership work, and of being interested in succeeding together at addressing upcoming challenges. While conventional wisdom says "the proof is in the pudding" (meaning "I'll start to trust them when they prove they can be trusted, which we all know will take [a long] time . . ."), a different dynamic emerges when the level and effectiveness of the conversation are rich enough. This new perspective and relationship might be characterized as "I recognize there are no guarantees when it comes to maintaining trust, but I have a sense that we are sincere about working as partners to achieve a common aim. I am satisfied we have a framework that is best able to support the intention of building a trusting partnership together, and I am looking forward to the opportunity this relationship presents."

While it is true that behavior that led to the mistrust must change or else this new perspective will rapidly deteriorate, both parties should give up the right to play "gotcha." As we often say, your job is to "cause it rather than expect it." There is no room for catching each other's missteps inside a context of partnership. Without doubt, there will be slip-ups and setbacks. But in a context of partnership, these can be dealt with in ways that deepen and strengthen the overall level of trust. Periodically revisiting the trust assessment matrix

Trust Component	Decrease Trust	Maintain Trust	Increase Trust
Being Honest	Lie, misrepresent, hide, withhold, omit. Have hidden agendas. Conceal intent. Gossip and undermine others. Make commitments without intending to fulfill them. Generate rumors and misunderstandings. Create conspiracies and collusion.	Tell the truth. Say what you mean and mean what you say. Be as open as necessary to maintain the trust. Walk your talk. Don't hide behind corporate direction or strategy.	Be vulnerable and authentic. Express concerns. Pursue the truth even when uncomfortable. Confront issues directly and openly. Announce intentions clearly and unequivocally. Stand on principles, not popularity. Insist that others' intentions are clear and explicit.
Being Dependable	Miss deadlines and commitments. Fall short of deliverables without warning. Be inconsistent and full of excuses.	Consistently deliver on promises. Communicate ahead of time regarding shortfalls. Update others on promises before they have to ask for follow-up. Take ownership of decisions.	Initiate offers beyond what is requested—and deliver. Manage the promises of others. Be impeccably reliable. Support others to be dependable.
Exercising Judgment	Make promises without considering your ability to deliver. Make fantastic claims regarding deliverables and fall short—then blame others or circumstances.	Make and deliver on promises consistent with your demonstrated skills and abilities. Offer advice and information only in your areas of expertise.	Consistently expand your abilities and expertise consistent with larger promises. Demonstrate the ability to make and deliver on bold promises. Bring the right parties to the right conversations for decisions. Keep the right people informed and included, in the right way and time.
Generating Partnership	Ignore the impact of your actions on others. Look out for yourself only. Ignore the concerns and feelings of others. Be self-centered.	Take the concerns and feelings of others into account. Check on others' reactions before deciding a course of action.	Genuinely listen to and collaborate with others. Elicit support and alignment from others. Seek ways to ensure others are included and respected. Own others' success.

Figure 7-3. Behaviors that increase or decrease trust.

and initiating ongoing dialogue will provide a framework to continuously expand and deepen trust among the parties.

It *is* possible to view past events from new perspectives, and to set about designing new relationship dynamics that account for the history but are not determined by it. We are not advocating blind trust or naive foolishness; after all, you would not ask your toddler to prepare your tax return, nor ask a student in a beginning pilot's class to land on an aircraft carrier.

Our central claim is that breakdowns in trust can be systematically identified, addressed, and transformed into opportunities for partnership and growth. There are no shortcuts here and no guarantees. Building trust can be a tedious and arduous process, replete with setbacks, frustration, resignation, and irritation. Cutting ourselves off from those with whom trust has been broken may seem the most attractive option, and in some cases it may be a legitimate course of action. But when the overall intent is to build an environment of strategic commitment—a culture of total alignment and engagement—giving up is not an option.

♦ ♦ ♦

CHAPTER 8

RETURN ON STRATEGIC COMMITMENT

On Competitive Edge and Profit Margins

There is no excuse for undertaking any major strategic change without expecting a return on that investment, and investing in generating strategic commitment is no exception.

In fact, when strategic commitment is present, we have consistently seen extraordinary results in key categories such as 1) financial performance, 2) customer service, satisfaction, and loyalty, 3) quality, 4) safety, 5) innovation, 6) cross-functional collaboration, 7) mergers and acquisitions, and 8) employee morale, loyalty, and satisfaction. Let's look at examples of results in each of these categories.

Financial Performance

No one in their right mind will dispute that revenues, expenses, profits, and EBITDA are the most important metrics for a CEO and his leadership to drive and manage. Despite that fact, financial metrics are often paid lip service to because of internal politics, personal agendas, self-interests, and egos. People often play games with the numbers (we don't mean in a criminal way). For example, sales groups achieve their quota before the end of the quarter and delay deals until the following quarter, even if other departments are behind and the overall sales results of the company are in question. There is often tension and fights between sales and operations about budgets. When budgets are overrun, each blames the other for being the source of it. Another example: In some organizations, even when cost-cutting measures are announced, people find ways to get away with spending money that isn't for mission-critical activities.

Issues such as these are more easily transformed in an environment of strategic commitment. When people take ownership and accountability and start thinking about themselves as owners of the business, they actually begin to do the right things with greater passion and determination. When Jim Burns (whom we introduced in chapter 4) elevated his telecommunications company leadership team, he was able to step back and relinquish control of the weekly sales objectives. At first it was touch-and-go, but after a very short period his leaders took the game on and ensured that the numbers were delivered without him. When people truly commit, they stop paying lip service and start being obsessed with how to make things work.

Some years ago, the private clients group at Fleet Bank (now part of Bank of America) held regular meetings with all 400 officers charged with managing the bank's largest customers. The intent was not only to share strategy and best practices, but to ensure that both content and context drivers were uniform: one message from one voice (the executive in charge). As a result of these sessions, they were able to access resources readily so that there was one point of contact per customer; retain top customers and increase word-of-mouth marketing and referrals; and become much more proactive in suggesting new products and services.

Customer Service, Satisfaction, and Loyalty

On the way to a business appointment, we recently stopped for gas at a service station, and—reluctantly—asked for the keys to the washroom as nature was calling. Dreading the unsanitary unpleasantness most often associated with these locales, we were more than pleased to find a clean, nicely-cared-for facility. So pleased, in fact, that we went out of our way to compliment the attendant on how spotless things were. His response: "Yes, I make sure the washrooms are clean because that's the way I like them, and I want our customers to feel good about using them." We asked how long he had owned the operation, and to our surprise he said, "I just work here. I'm not the owner." No question we'll return to that service station again, and not just when we need to use the washroom.

Contrast that example with that of a global manufacturer with a near-monopoly in its major product line. This company steadily lost market share as a result of internecine turf battles between the sales, operations, and quality units. While leaders of these groups preached about the need for handling customer complaints rapidly and thoroughly to drive customer satisfaction, the behind-the-scenes finger-pointing, blaming, and fault-finding left customers with chronic, unresolved issues and deeply *dissatisfied*. This lack of alignment, trust, and open and honest communication led directly to competitors stealing significant business.

We have always been impressed with the way in which Enterprise Rent-a-Car raced past Hertz as the largest such service provider. The key to its success was delivering to customers and moving into communities (not just offering service at airports). Enterprise entrepreneurs were busy serving neighborhoods and the people you see regularly in the community. You now see Hertz following suit, but as a late-comer, far after the fact.

Creating an environment of strategic commitment allows organizations to create an across-the-board obsession with satisfying customers and increasing customer loyalty, and as a result, they spend far less on customer acquisition and beat their competitors by generating more dollars of revenue from customers they already have.

Quality

Toyota implements 5,000 employee ideas a week and runs some of the safest operations in the world. They have overtaken General Motors not merely as a function of having better-designed vehicles, but by having products that customers know are reliable and employees who take ownership rather than act out of mere compliance. Companies that generate an environment of strategic commitment begin to elevate awareness and embed quality in everything they do.

As part of his strategic plan for 2006, Merlin Industries' president Andrew Maggion aligned his management team around a commitment to "impeccable fulfillment" of customer orders. Merlin—a Hamilton, New Jersey-based manufacturer of pool and spa covers and vinyl liners—had always enjoyed a good reputation with customers, but Andy and his team were convinced they could significantly reduce customer complaints and order-to-delivery turnaround times by improving the quality of their work.

After quickly analyzing the source of quality-related complaints, the champion of the quality initiative rallied all managers to make the reduction of defects a priority. He, with Andy's close support and involvement, educated the entire 200-person workforce on the large and small activities they performed on a daily basis that could impact quality. One simple example of an improvement they made: the Customer Service and Drafting groups had different standards for what constituted a complete order, and incomplete orders would sit unprocessed leading to delayed orders and frustrated customers. In the spirit of realizing their mutually agreed objective, the groups sat down, hashed out an agreement, and reduced their turnaround times significantly. Defects decreased dramatically, and Merlin enjoyed a healthy increase in business.

We were at a desultory conference and played hooky at the breakfast restaurant, where two bored hostesses oversaw the customers.

Once seated, we were about to call for the manager when we encountered Jose. He told a few jokes, tried out our Spanish, and steered us to the best choice of food. We told the manager later that the guy exemplified quality.

"We're all set with him," said the manager, beaming. "No," we said, "not until you get him to teach your hostesses and banquet staff his secrets."

Safety

Safe workplaces begin with a safety mind-set and attitude, not with safety programs. Everybody in his or her right mind would say that safety is paramount, yet people don't always act that way. We have seen instances where—in spite of the fact that safety was a declared top priority—the end of the quarter loomed with a predicted shortfall in production and obvious safety issues were overlooked in the name of "getting the product out the door at any cost." We've also encountered employees who are frustrated because they feel their supervisors are not listening to their safety-related concerns because they are more worried about production-driven compensation. When strategic commitment is present, communication is strong, real issues are talked about and addressed no matter how difficult, and people look out for each other and the good of the whole. In this environment—with people acting as owners of the business rather than passengers on someone else's bus—safety programs can be highly effective.

One of the key promises the management team at Augusta Newsprint made in their effort to become one of the top ten newsprint operations in the world was to lead their company in not only cost and quality metrics, but safety incidents as well.

Focus groups were conducted throughout to raise awareness around areas of safety risk, and brainstorming sessions were held to identify potential problems and address them proactively rather than waiting for something to happen.

The general manager (GM) was unwavering in his insistence that nothing preempted safe working practices, and the management team firmly believed they were on the right track.

Shockingly, a long-time employee was killed in a freak accident while repairing a major piece of equipment. Managers and employees alike were stunned; they had lost a friend and colleague due to a confluence of circumstances no one believed could have happened. But this only strengthened their commitment to safety.

Over the remainder of the year, employees were paying close attention to any and all safety-related issues. Managers were listening, caring, and highly responsive to issues employees raised, and the ever-possible tension between "get the product out the door" and "safety first" was well in hand.

At the first management team meeting of the New Year, the GM declared to his team they had won the corporate safety award. The team was jubilant—they had overcome the tragic events of 18 months before, and had won the game they had established for themselves. However, the story does not end here.

Later that week, the team discovered an employee with a bandage on his finger. As it turned out, he had been on shift New Year's eve and had received a fairly minor cut (before midnight) that he had failed to report to the infirmary as standard procedures dictated.

The GM and his team agreed that—given the environment of trust, honesty and collaboration they had created—they would report the incident based on when it happened, and forfeit their award. Rather than being demoralized by giving up the award, they yet again made their commitment to safety paramount.

In addition to dramatically improving all manufacturing performance areas that year, results against safety metrics soared.

Innovation

No company is more highly regarded for innovation these days than Apple, Inc. And while Steve Jobs has a reputation for being demanding and obsessed with details, he has created an environment within the company where people are dedicated to building "insanely great" products. This obsession with excellence and innovation is common in companies that generate strategic commitment. One can readily make the case that Apple generates more emotional attachment from its employees and customers than any other technology firm in the world, and more than almost any other firm you can think of.

3M Company, the 108-year-old industrial manufacturer that invented—among a list of hundreds of products—Scotchgard, Post-it Notes, and more recently Post-it Picture Paper, is another outstanding example. Key to 3M's success: maintaining a corporate culture that is consistent with the philosophy of William McKnight, its leader from 1929 to 1966. In his May 2006 *Business Week* article, "3M's Seven Pillars of Innovation," Michael Arndt notes that this culture is captured in McKnight's stated belief: "Hire good people and let them do their job in their own ways. And tolerate mistakes." Ensuring opportunities for networking among 3M researchers is key; every year all 9,700 R & D personnel attend a meeting to share ideas and learn about what is happening in other parts of the company. In addition, 3M's rewards system encourages development of discoveries that lead to real-world products. Employees are nominated and selected by their peers for scientific achievement awards every year, with the top twenty winners (and their spouses) given holidays at the company's corporate retreat. Management's unambiguous commitment to innovation, along with the financial and organizational systems to support objectives in that arena, clearly signal what is important at 3M.

The British Standards Institute was struggling with innovation and the threat from their new economic community "competitors."

After a week of live application of innovative ideas, the five teams we worked with there had ten solid suggestions to exponentially grow the influence and range of the Institute. The managing director came to Milton Keynes from London, listened passively for two hours, and then announced, "If these ideas are so bloody good, why hasn't anyone done them before?"

And that was the end of commitment at that organization.

Cross-Functional Collaboration

Many large and complex multinational companies operate with a highly matrixed management structure in which technology, operations, strategy, and regional groups must collaborate intensely to continue to lead the industry. Sergio Cunha (names in this example are fictionalized), VP of operations and planning for his company's European region, took over a group that operated in silos where country operations managers strongly identified themselves with their solid-line jobs but felt a weak sense of connection and loyalty to the region's functional heads. "I talked about us being a community and issued an eight-point plan that everyone seemed to agree with; however, getting people to come to our meetings—not to mention working on collective priorities—continued to be a struggle. It seemed that people were relating to the plan as mine, not theirs," he says.

Cunha, who came from managing a region in which everyone reported directly to him, was challenged with how to influence a group without line authority. Yet he was resolved to build a true community. With no small amount of persuasion, convincing and talking with people's bosses, he managed to get the entire group together for a face-to-face community kickoff session. This was a watershed event that allowed all managers to clear the air and commit to a shared purpose and objectives for the community. This new sense of collective purpose and ownership allowed people to break down the silos, stop worrying about who they reported to, and start collaborating on how to add greater value to their customers. According to one sales representative from the United Kingdom, "I was probably the most skeptical about the potential value of this group. Historically, we did not feel this forum could be of any help to us. We now have developed a strong sense of community, and the value we're providing each other is directly benefiting our customers."

Integration of Cultures (Mergers and Acquisitions)

Failed mergers and unmet expectations from acquisitions are more the norm than the exception. Getting everyone from both sides of a merger or acquisition to be on the same page about the direction of the new entity, and working side-by-side to produce a one-plus-one-equals-122 outcome, is the prize all executives are hoping for. Strategic commitment is the condition that allows for that to happen. In most M & A situations, the focus is primarily on integrating the roles and functions *on paper*. When it comes time to execute, companies find it extremely challenging (just follow the track record) to actually integrate and merge people's minds and hearts. People know very well how to "go along," "play the game," "pretend," and "go through the motions." When they do that, they find ways to do the least, sometimes even undermining the M & A effort while appearing like they are really on board. The game gets decided at the shop floor level, not the high conceptual level.

In May of 2003, Insurance behemoth Prudential Financial acquired the U.S. operations of Sweden's Skandia Insurance Co. Ltd. in a $1.2 billion move. The president of Prudential's Annuities group at the time made it clear from the outset he wanted to combine the best both organizations had to offer. Rather than pay lip service to this "best of both" principle—as many acquirers often do—he followed through on his intent and ensured his leaders did the same.

Right off the bat, he gathered his new team of direct reports, which included proportional representation from the new and old organizations, and set out to establish a new shared compelling vision for the organization, one that both parties could find themselves in. He drove a leadership team culture of openness, honesty, and absolute collaboration; finger-pointing and empire building were not tolerated. Says one leadership team member, "The partnership between the Risk, Product, Investment, Marketing and Actuarial teams became excellent. We (Skandia and Prudential) agreed very quickly on the key few ways we were going to succeed. We had a clear strategic intent right from the get go; and we were very honest with each other when things were not working."

Another leadership team member says, "Relationship building has been very good; that's gone a really long way in working with other areas so they try and find solutions. Our partnership with the Actuarial group in testing, bringing projects to implementation, and developing products that people want is a very collaborative and constructive process."

On a regular basis, the business unit leader made presentations to all employees to help them understand the risks the group faced, the competition they were up against, and their progress toward organizational objectives.

Perhaps summing up the entire acquisition best is the head of product development: "Five years ago we were two different cultures—Prudential and Skandia. I've seen many companies struggle with acquisitions before. This time we melded two organizations; Skandia people took the sales, marketing and product roles, and Prudential people took the operations, risk, and actuarial roles. Now it's 1/3, 1/3, 1/3, part Prudential, part Skandia, and part new. We ended up with a unique culture that brought out the best in everyone. Traditional M&A is 'who won, who lost?' We're way beyond that here."

The buzz in the industry is that Prudential Annuities is innovative, expanding, and extremely successful.

More than 80 percent of mergers and acquisitions are unsuccessful. One of the most spectacular failures was the Mercedes takeover of Chrysler, which the top executives of Daimler-Benz began to brag about—something odd for a "merger of equals." Quite rapidly, top talent was lost, market share was lost, and profits plummeted at Chrysler. Now divested and sold, Chrysler is a shadow of its former self. Mercedes management didn't seem to care a hoot about strategic commitment and crafted one of the greatest losses in their storied history.

> **StratComment**
>
> *Strategic commitment is optimally the common "cement" that can bind two cultures in the aftermath of a merger and acquisition.*

Employee Morale, Loyalty, and Satisfaction

Conventional wisdom tells us that employee morale suffers when circumstances require cost-cutting or layoffs, or in times of economic downturns. We don't believe that's true. The health of employee satisfaction is directly linked to *how* managers address these situations. In fact, we have seen numerous examples of companies employing strategic commitment in difficult times where morale and employee satisfaction increased.

A VP of Sales within a large consumer packaged goods company faced the need to reduce his group size by 40 percent, given competitive pressures on his company. Rather than succumbing to the inevitable demoralization of his group, he rallied his leaders to stand for a bold, innovative outcome of *raising* employee satisfaction while reducing the size of the workforce. Rather than the traditional and secretive closed-door approach to this type of process, they went out of their way to be open and transparent about all decisions and consequences. They formed a committee whose sole purpose was to find new positions (inside or outside the company) for those whose jobs were being eliminated, ensuring people felt respected and cared for. As a consequence of these and other activities, they increased employee satisfaction by 50 percent during this time period—a re-markable outcome.

Terry Sampson (name fictionalized in this example), Director of Safety Operations for a global pharmaceutical company, created a bold vision with his team. Over the course of a year, they focused on partnering more effectively with each other and building trust between departments in order to better serve their customers. They kept each other well informed about projects being worked on by groups in separate locations, and created a newsletter aimed at shar-ing knowledge between groups and increasing their sense of shared purpose and community. They aligned all of their work with the over-arching vision and key objectives. The group significantly improved employee satisfaction (they moved from 3.05 to 3.29 as measured by the Gallup Q12 instrument—a dramatic improvement according to Gallup) as well as customer satisfaction, and their own in-ternal "team health" scores.

> **StratComment**
>
> *Strategic commitment actually enhances the return in all areas of per-formance.*

These are just two of many examples we have seen firsthand of organizations that— in the pursuit of strategic commitment—elevated key employee and culture metrics.

The Drivers Working Every Day

The American Institute of Architects (AIA) is not a licensing body, but a non-profit membership group. Although headquartered in Washington, D.C., it has neither regulatory power nor certifica-tion authority. (Architects are registered by the states in which they practice.)

Working with them some years ago, we noted some fascinating dynamics consistent with strategic commitment.

Only about half of the 100,000 architects in the United States are actually members, but they are all entitled to use "AIA" after their names. Many customers, stakeholders, and even related professionals (e.g., designers, general contractors) often mistake that designation for a higher degree of competency.

Augmenting its aura of prominence, the AIA publishes research, provides design templates, conducts workshops, holds an annual convention, supports local chapters, and publishes magazines, even awarding a prestigious honor yearly to an outstanding architect any-where in the world (who need not be an AIA member). Membership ranges from large firms to solo practitioners.

The AIA board actively solicits input from its diverse member-ship base and employees (many of whom originated in the profession, especially at management level). Thus, we have a trade association that achieves great loyalty and leverages the status of membership by aligning itself closely with the needs of the membership, and conversely expects the membership to par-ticipate in its strategy and implementation. The board of fifty-plus officers (an other-wise unwieldy number that can produce contentiousness) provides enormously di-verse input to the organization's direction and carries back this involvement to local state chapters.

> **StratComment**
>
> *Prestige and repute are strong returns from ef-fective strategic commit-ment.*

When Strategic Planning Meets Strategic Commitment

The approach taken in developing a strategic plan has everything to do with generating strategic commitment within the organiza-tion. As discussed in chapter 3, there are many different methods for articulating the content of a strategy: Vision, mission, BHAG (big, hairy, audacious goals), best-in-class, strategic intent—to mention a few of the popular ones—they can all be effective methods depending on how they are applied. There are two fun-damentally different approaches, however, to applying any of these methods: one that is fundamentally grounded in and driven by history, and one that is grounded in, and driven by a desired future state.

In traditional strategic planning processes, organizations analyze their own past performance, while also benchmarking the performance of their competitors and the marketplace. Assumptions and conclusions are derived from this analysis that indicate what is realistic, best case, and worst case for the organization in the future. In this commonly used, lengthy approach (shown in Figure 8-1), the boldness and ambition of the strategy is determined and constrained by historical trends.

We side with more modern business thinkers who suggest a fundamentally different approach to strategy. They believe that while it is important to learn from your own as well as your competitors' and markets' historical performance, it is equally (if not more) important for an organization to be able to take a well-informed and responsible stand about where it is headed, commit to it, and then put all the necessary structures, initiatives, resources, and accountabilities in place to ensure its success. This approach draws the line between adopting an unrealistic strategy (which leaders might get excited about in the moment of creation, only to find themselves overwhelmed and discouraged by its implementation) and taking on a bold and aggressive strategy that is informed but not determined by historical performance—a realistic breakthrough. The future-based strategies require the organization to break new ground, think outside the box, and do things that they had never done before in order to fulfill those strategies. Contrary to the traditional approach, which is often done by a small committee, this approach can only be achieved through a process in which the team engages in deep and meaningful dialogue about the current situation, issues, opportunities, and desires. It is a dialogue in which choices are made, stands are taken, and commitments are aligned on, in real time, without unnecessary delay, "analysis paralysis," and procrastination.

We propose a strategic planning method that leverages the prin-

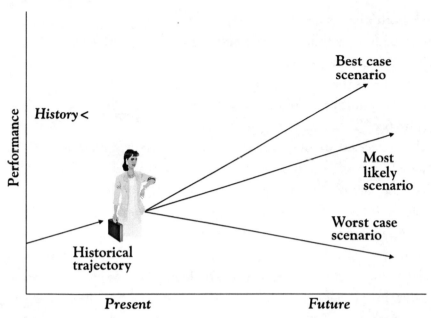

Figure 8-1. *Traditional strategic planning: grounded in and driven by history.*

ciples and language of strategic commitment and hence can be used exactly in the way we outline below, or can serve as guiding principles for whatever method you choose.

A Strategic Plan Fit for Strategic Commitment

"Commitment" has a dual meaning:

1. A *declaration*: "I am committed to a cause." It captures an inspirational future. It is a statement that shapes and establishes one's personal platform, vision, and relationship to an idea or possibility. Action is implied, but not explicit; describable but not measurable.

2. A *promise*: "I commit to an action or deliverable outcome." You can only commit to a specific and measurable outcome, result, or action. Plus, a promise must have a clear time frame for delivery. In the case of a promise, action and deliverables are explicit, not implicit.

Both dimensions of a commitment are critical, and without them something will be missing. (They are two halves of a whole, two aspects that make the magic happen.)

> **StratComment**
>
> *There are two types of commitment. One is from the heart, the other from the mind.*

A commitment to a direction can inspire people, but without tangible deliverables success cannot be measured, and people can become cynical. People may get excited about the direction and what is being built, but they are not effectively focused on action and results to actually deliver it (no promise, no results).

At the same time, promising results without a compelling vision or purpose can leave people trying to meet objectives without understanding and connecting with the bigger picture of what is being built. People get bogged down with activities without looking at the bigger picture, so they neglect to constantly evaluate opportunities to work smarter rather than harder. In this mode, people just "go, go, go." They are good compliers but not necessarily good strategic thinkers. They march lockstep, but have no care about the direction.

In light of the dual meaning of commitment, we propose a framework that includes a strategic vision, strategic promises, and a process for generating both.

- □ *Strategic vision* refers to a clear and concise articulation of the future that captures the essence of what the organization is aiming to become and deliver. This statement meets these criteria:

    a. Expresses a future condition in the present tense. ("*We are* . . . ," not "We will be. . . .")

    b. Is bold, audacious, and compelling. It requires a realistic breakthrough in organizational behavior in order for the vision to be realized.

    c. Expresses *what* you will achieve, not *how* you will achieve it. It may well be something you don't fully know how to achieve when creating it.

d. Establishes a unique identity. It is not something *any* organization could say.

e. Allows everyone in the organization to connect to it. The statement is narrow enough to have everyone march in the same direction, and at the same time it allows for personal expressions, interpretations, and behaviors.

◻ *Strategic promises* are the few key measurable outcomes that will be used to objectively determine success for the organization. These promises:

a. Must be measurable or clearly describable ("We will achieve a 4 percent expense-to-revenue ratio," not "We will improve expense management"). These metrics may already exist or they can be invented.

b. Answer the question, "What must we *achieve?*" (not "What must we *do?*"), so everyone will know when we have realized the vision. Again, it represents the *what*, not the *how*.

c. Must represent a realistic breakthrough from history. Strategic promises should be exciting and compelling.

d. Are always stated as outcomes, not processes ("We want 90 percent customer satisfaction with our speed of response," not "We need to increase our speed of response so that customers are satisfied"). These are the ends, not the means.

e. Should be a total of three to six, not a list of every project that is important.

f. Address each explicit and/or implicit area in which the strategic vision establishes a need for a realistic breakthrough. For example, if the statement specifies improvements in speed, customer satisfaction, employee teamwork, and innovation, these areas must be accounted for within the strategic promises.

g. Are promises, not priorities. By this we mean that they are all equal in importance, rather than priorities that are ranked and get addressed in order of importance (hence, working on priority 5 only happens if there is time or capacity left from working on priority 4). In contrast, promises are taken on with equal priority, which often requires greater innovation to ensure they are all met, especially when resources are scarce.

- *The process* of generating a strategic vision and strategic promises is extremely important. Here are some key principles to pay attention to:

  a. An open and honest environment is essential. Teams should not engage in a strategy discussion before they have sufficient trust in the openness, honesty, authenticity, and courage of their conversations.

  b. A state of total alignment, not consensus, is required (as discussed in chapter 3). This alignment is driven by a clear understanding that there must be complete buy-in and ownership within the leadership group crafting the vision and promises. This alignment will form the basis for a powerful starting place to begin to deliver the desired future state.

  c. The dialogue requires rigor, discipline, focus, and drive combined with *patience*. People need to recognize that "fast is slow."

> **StratComment**
> *The old West Point and army advisory, "Hurry up and wait," might not be bad advice in many instances.*

Doing It Right

Here are some additional and powerful guidelines when crafting the strategic vision and promises:

- *Stay oriented around the future state.* It's about getting the team to totally own and identify with the future state, not about getting sexy words on paper.

- *Take the time to ensure that people truly know what they are talking about* before trying to figure out how to come up with slogans and fancy phrases. We constantly find that people are so jaded (from so many strategic planning exercises!) that everything seems like everything else. So people often get stuck on a word or phrase because they haven't sufficiently discussed and generated clarity and alignment around what they are really trying to say. Generally, we have found that people lack the patience and rigor to articulate things at a level that truly distinguishes new ideas and commitments. Instead, everything is general and vague.

- *Be rigorous.* Don't let people's lack of patience and tolerance determine the depth of the dialogue. Actually spend the time necessary to drive clarity and authentic alignment; it will pay off in implementation.

- Remember that *there are no true or false, right or wrong answers,* only choices to be made by the leaders (that is their job) and being fully responsible for those choices.

- *Focus on progress not perfection!* It's about movement, not the ideal. When people surrender to the process it is magical.

- *Consult experts when necessary.* We have talked a lot about using outside expertise for content of the strategy. To get the most out of outside consultants and experts, remember the biggest rule is that you must always own the process and outcome (you learn to fish rather than merely receive more fishes). We advise all our clients to never (*never!*) abdicate that core responsibility. There may be areas where you are not the expert or don't have all the information or the best information. However, it is always *your* business, your game to elevate, your achievement, your success or failure. Never just "go along for the ride" or believe that because they are the experts they will blindly lead you.

□ *Use and/or call in your HR leaders and experts as needed.* But if you do that, you have to make sure they can and will take the game to the next level. In our next chapter, we discuss the historical and future roles of human resources. Our perspective is that HR should "lead, follow, or get out of the way."

We stood in the main corridor of headquarters once with Lowell Anderson when he was president of Allianz Life Insurance in Minneapolis. He had just announced a $100 bonus for every person who was outside of the senior management bonus system. It had been a great year, achieved only through outstanding strategic commitment, and we had agreed that the $35,000 or so was a great investment. While not a huge amount of money, it was a nice gesture—and just in time for Christmas shopping.

In no time at all, we saw elevators open, stairwell doors fly open, and every access way disgorge people who were headed toward human resources to claim their small "windfall." Many people stopped just long enough to say "Thank you" to Lowell, who was grinning from ear to ear.

We knew that the return on this simple investment in commitment would be paying dividends for the foreseeable future. Where are you spending that hundred bucks?

CHAPTER 9

◆ ◆ ◆

LEAD, FOLLOW, OR GET OUT OF THE WAY–HR AT THE CROSSROADS

The Role of HR in Generating Strategic Commitment

Can HR actually help? Based on history, no! Our experience shows that if you go to most companies and gauge internal functions and lines of business (human resources' customers) in an informal honest conversation about their perceptions of the HR department, they will often describe HR in unfavorable terms, as "difficult to deal with, a necessary evil, inflexible, complex, academic, out of touch, focused on its own agenda, political, weak and ineffective, not customer-oriented, irrelevant," or as a department that "doesn't understand our business, and is helpful mainly (or only) on technical or compliance-related items."

Other than that, they're great! It shouldn't be a shock that the overall reputation of human resources in most companies is a low one. HR is often considered old-fashioned, bureaucratic, and cumbersome to deal with. (Name three Fortune 500 firms that have promoted an HR executive to CEO in the past ten years. You can't.)

To Be or Not to Be:
Can Your Human Resources People Actually Help?

We have also asked many HR managers how *they* feel about and view their own function, and in many cases they see things the same way, even though we hear desires within the HR community of being "strategic partners" and "having a seat at the table." For the most part, HR managers' own self-image, self-esteem, and expectations are not very high. And in most situations, despite their declarations and intentions to the contrary, HR managers are resigned to the possibility that this may be as good as it gets.

For some HR departments, this *is* as good as it gets. Other HR managers, however, are frustrated because

> **StratComment**
>
> *HR is no longer a transactional function, since these aspects have been largely outsourced for good economic reasons. That leaves open the possibility of HR performing a transformational function, which requires credibility, talent, and courage—qualities not historically the strong suit of HR professionals.*

they want a more robust, high impact, and valuable role in their organization. They want to make a bigger difference, and they feel stuck because they don't know how to change their predicament, or else they feel their stakeholders and customers won't allow and trust them to play a more important role.

At the lower levels of the HR team, these frustrations are often heightened. The frustration is often directed toward the HR leaders, whom lower-level managers blame for not having the courage, foresight, and commitment to elevate themselves and their function to a higher, more influential, and meaningful role.

It's a bromide that every HR executive wants to be in the innermost circle of top management. Yet few of them are. They may have a title—executive vice president, senior vice president, or director—that puts them on par with their counterparts in strategy, finance, marketing, sales, R & D, manufacturing, and distribution.

But that title alone doesn't actually make the HR leader the strategic partner of the CEO and other executive team members. In fact, we have seen instances where the HR leader was not invited by the CEO to participate in important strategic meetings and conversations that the CEO was holding with key business and functional leaders (peers of the HR leader). No mystery here. This is consistent with the historical paradigm described above.

Even when opportunities exist that could be ideal for HR to step up and provide leadership, such as when organizations suffer from a toxic political environment that undermines and prevents strategic commitment, in many cases HR leaders don't. They opine about, and often complain about, the issues, which only contributes to the problem. At times HR may help by bringing in external professionals, but mostly it continues to be viewed as the benefits administrator and watchdog over hiring, promotion, compensation, and other people practices, and it is infrequently a significant player in shaping the overall company strategy.

HR for the most part is trapped in a vicious circle that keeps reinforcing itself. It wants to elevate its status and value but is challenged first and foremost by it own historical model. Simply said, it is hard for HR professionals, starting with the senior ones, to change their own mind-set and self-image in order to become more courageous and influential. The more HR wants to operate outside this predicament (to become transformational), the more customers are skeptical because they only expect more of the same and view HR as incapable of providing more.

This predicament makes it ever harder for HR to metamorphose.

HR as Chief Commitment Officer: The Best of All Possible Worlds?

So, can HR really step up and transform itself to become a key driver of change and improvement in the organization? Can HR ever be perceived by the CEO and all key stakeholders and customers as one of the most important and influential drivers of the success of the organization? The answer is an emphatic Yes!

HR is not powerless to transform attitude problems that have emanated from even the highest levels of the organization. Toxic environments and a lack of strategic commitment are not the *fault of HR*, however they can become the *responsibility of HR* to transform and fix. HR is far better positioned than any other function to help the CEO and top executives gel, and then get the rest of the company on board with their direction.

Furthermore, if HR executives assume this responsibility, they can elevate their impact—and that of the HR function—to an entirely new level. It's a level beyond the one played by most HR executives today.

We realize this might sound implausible. An HR executive reversing many years of deep organizational dysfunctionality and dissent? The HR head getting all members of the executive team to devote themselves to one another and the CEO, and vice versa? It is hard to fathom. But we have seen HR executives who are playing such a role in their organizations. They (increasingly) see themselves as "chief commitment officers" because they are the key players behind the scenes helping the CEO gain internal commitment to the company's strategic direction and initiatives.

StratComment

Ironically, employees often least committed and included historically in organizational change and improvement can become the chief commitment sources in the future. HR can transform its reputation by getting these people on board.

Any HR leader can play this role, no matter how toxic the corporate culture, if the leader musters the courage and conviction to do so and learns the rules, steps, and boundaries of the game. In fact, we propose HR leaders *must* do so. This is their imperative of the day. It won't be easy or painless, and it won't happen overnight, but it is the only way they will be able to elevate themselves and their organization to a new level of impact, value, and reputation.

"HR executives today need to play a much more important role at the top of their companies, more than hiring and securing the right skills," says Monica Woods (name fictionalized) from one of the world's largest networking companies. "Hiring the best talent to fuel our growth is definitely critical; however, as an HR leader, I cannot only focus on getting talent in the door. Perhaps my most important job is to ensure that senior management creates an environment that helps our people achieve exceptional performance."

This isn't strictly a modern phenomenon. HR executives Art Strohmer and Steve Darien, now retired, led Merck as it was named America's Most Admired Company five consecutive times. Marilyn Martiny, now retired, worked in knowledge management at Hewlett-Packard and absolutely was a catalyst for line managers to transform the organization. The problem is that it is so easy to choose these exceptions from the vast HR community.

Building Potential: HR Can Help, but Needs Your Help

HR can become *the* driver of change, but only if the CEO truly owns the process. This qualifier might be heard as a condition and excuse: "We can only do it *if* the CEO enables us." In fact, we hear many HR leaders excuse their lack of impact by claiming a lack of CEO support and endorsement. We don't mean it this way at all. Yes, it takes two to tango. However, it takes one to initiate the tango, and the one in this case is HR.

The CEO must personally own the process of building an open, honest, and sincere environment. However, it is the role of HR to coach and enroll the CEO in that recognition and belief.

We have already mentioned how in many companies the CEO

views people and cultural issues as matters that are less mission-critical than the financial metrics, therefore the CEO outsources or delegates that "people stuff" to the HR leader. Some HR leaders actually like that because it makes them feel more important. This is flawed thinking because they fail to see that their ability to truly transform toxic and dysfunctional politics is going to be stifled unless people feel the CEO fully owns that intent. The most powerful HR leaders we have seen are those who have been able to quickly detect toxic issues—the backstabbing, the victim mentality, finger pointing, and turfism—and their impact on performance and productivity, and then effectively get the CEO to see, own, and act upon them. Sometimes it is easy to get leaders to own the dysfunctional dynamics around them because there are clear indicators, such as managers not achieving deliverables or receiving low scores on employee surveys.

At other times, however, it takes real courage and determination from the HR leaders to get through, especially when their leaders are out of touch or arrogant.

Senior VP Drew Moran, head of the Worldwide Channels group for a large networking company (all names in this example are fictionalized), faced the challenge

> ### StratComment
> *If the CEO doesn't trust HR, then HR might as well be eliminated. It either leads strategic commitment or it hinders it. There is no room in between.*

of significantly growing the company's partner/distributor-based sales. To build the necessary foundation for accelerated growth, Moran needed to get technology, functional, and regional groups—all reporting to different heads in a matrixed management model—to collaborate in a much more seamless and effective fashion.

Monica Woods, Moran's HR head, took on the role of being his full partner in driving this transformation. In spite of being new in her role at the time, she built significant credibility by spending the first few months on the job listening intently to the issues, needs, and concerns of her leadership peers.

She quickly recognized that departments, functions, and regional teams that needed to work together were not. Trust was lacking, communication was ineffective, and despite the fact that direction and priorities were set at the senior team, they were not operating with a common, shared purpose.

Woods was unwavering in her focus and determination to get the leadership team to recognize the depth of the problems and incite them to commit to change, which was challenging at times due to the individual and collective success the group had historically enjoyed.

"While I knew it was the right thing to do, I was tentative at first. As a newcomer to the business, I did not have the knowledge and background my business partners had. And they were unaccustomed to an HR leader playing the role I was taking on," says Woods.

She took it upon herself to initiate and participate in team sessions with many of her colleagues aimed at raising and addressing the tough and meaningful context issues. She helped the leaders begin to generate a new environment of honesty, trust, and collaboration within their teams, as well as between their teams and other groups.

"After a few successes, I felt more able and confident—plus, there was more receptivity on the part of other previously skeptical leaders to achieve the same within their groups," says Woods, who is now fully accepted as the chief commitment officer for Moran's organization. "We have extremely talented and effective executives among Moran's leadership team. However, when we would come together, many of us felt that the discussion was not as open, productive, and effective as it needed to be. We still have a ways to go, but the situation has changed dramatically by raising and addressing context issues."

I Won't Dance, Don't Ask Me: Jettisoning HR as an Impediment

So, what does HR's role look like when it is empowered properly?

In many organizations, CEOs often ask the HR chief to help them generate internal commitment to their strategies. The problem is that HR executives are only asked to assist with half of what it takes to gain substantial employee commitment—namely, the content drivers of the strategy. HR is typically asked to determine the people impact of the strategy. For example, if it is a cost-cutting initiative, how many heads should be cut to achieve the target, and how much layoff compensation must the company prepare to dispense? HR is also often (but not always) asked to then help leaders communicate the strategy to employees at all levels given that HR can be a good sounding board for what messages will resonate with or offend the masses.

But this is where HR's involvement in generating strategic commitment usually ends. As we've said repeatedly in earlier chapters, the other half (and the more critical one) of what it takes for a CEO to gain commitment to his strategy is attending to the *context* drivers: to repeat, workers' and managers' feelings toward their leaders' *sincerity and honesty* about what's really going on in the company, their *courage and resolve* to hear the truth and make the hard decisions required for the strategy to work, their *competence* in directing the strategic initiative at hand, and their *concern* for those who will be affected by it.

The role of the HR leader as chief commitment officer is to make the CEO aware of how he is perceived by his leadership team, especially in these four categories, and how the leadership team is perceived by their direct reports and so on, down through the entire organization.

The perceptions held by the executive team about the CEO and by the rest of the organization about the executive team are the most important ones for the HR executive to bring forth to the top boss. The CEO must understand what prevents top team members and other employees from getting fully behind him and the plan. Is it people's doubts about the CEO's willingness to deal with a key executive who isn't pulling his weight and is holding the organization back? Is it the failed strategic initiatives of a predecessor that is causing people to think, "Not again"? Is it their fear of suggesting process improvements that will streamline themselves out of their jobs? Is it their fear of how the CEO will react to criticism about his style or approach? The HR executive must also coach the CEO not to take the lack of commitment feedback personally. If the CEO reacts badly to hearing about a commitment problem, he will in fact only make it worse. The commitment problem can be fixed relatively quickly, but only if the CEO and the management team can trace the roots back to themselves, acknowledge it, and are willing to fix it.

The HR leader must also get executive team members to confront the negative

> **StratComment**
>
> *HR can be the vital communications and verification pipeline to ensure that both content and context drivers are being fully developed, understood, appreciated, and addressed.*

perceptions they have about one another, such as grudges, lack of personal and professional respect, and other attitudes that prevent people from trusting one another and working collaboratively. *In sum, the chief commitment officer must help executives understand and confront what prevents their underlings from embracing their plans.*

The HR executive needs to ensure that the hallway conversations are brought to the fore and addressed. Their role is to facilitate a dialogue and process in which colleagues and the boss are honest about the issues that are holding them back so that they can fully own and address them.

Executive team members must be permitted to vent their perceptions about others, even the comments that are hardest to hear (e.g., "marketing never meets its deadlines," "sales lies to potential customers just to close the deal," or "customer service screws up all the time"). Criticisms about the CEO, if warranted, must also be voiced. The HR executive must help the CEO create a safe environment in which no retribution will come to those who speak up—*especially about the CEO's behavior.*

This process can be uncomfortable and even emotional at times. But it will always be liberating and productive when done effectively.

Until executives can be truly honest with one another about their perceptions and where each of them may be falling short, they won't ever click. Frustrations and resentments will continue to undermine communication, alignment, trust, and partnership. The executive team members will fulfill their professional responsibilities, for sure. But they won't go to extraordinary lengths to do so. Often, coaching peers is more challenging than coaching one's boss. It can be perceived as trying to get ahead with the CEO. Therefore, the risk of being marginalized is quite high. "The HR leader must tread a fine line of being the coach for the entire team and on *no one's* side, neither the executive's nor his or her direct reports," says Monica Woods.

Jim Burns (mentioned previously in chapter 6), transformed his personal leadership style and generated tremendous growth for his business division over the last five years, but he also had significant help from his HR director, Peter McNally.

"Early on in our transformation initiative, Peter took ownership and initiative way beyond the traditional HR support role," says Burns. "He was continuously in my face, providing blunt feedback about where I was acting consistent with my commitment to build an open, honest environment, and where I was falling short. I'm not the easiest guy to coach, but he didn't give up, and I admire his courage and appreciated his valuable insight and contribution. No question it made us closer."

McNally helped the team become more collaborative and team-oriented by working with his colleagues in meetings and behind the scenes to eliminate background noise and get them comfortable dealing directly with each other. He also partnered with each of his colleagues to design and facilitate processes with their respective teams to cascade the open, direct culture they were building.

He became the champion for the strategic promise of "Making the U.K. an extraordinary place to work," which was aimed at getting all employees to embrace a shared vision for the business unit. In that capacity, he was instrumental in getting all management layers on the same page about the shared vision. He was also relentless—"in our face," as Bob Kernan (U.K. head of sales) says, about "insisting that we take on making our employees feel cared for, which was addressing one of the areas we were weakest at, based on our previous pulse survey."

Says McNally, "The reason I chose this field is because I always believed the true opportunity of HR is to build extraordinary work environments for people; this is what most inspires me. It's all about people—how to inspire, motivate, empower, and engage them. Yes, we need to manage and administer the myriad of processes and policies that go with the territory HR has always held. However, we mustn't forget that the real prize is getting people fully energized to deliver their best."

Surprisingly, many HR leaders, according to our experience, struggle with assessing their organizational condition. They often minimize, sugarcoat, or reduce the severity of dysfunctional dynamics, concerned that it may imply that they are not doing their jobs properly. And they often seem to be somewhat out of touch with the context issues in their organizations, either because they are overly internally focused on traditional HR activities or simply don't

StratComment
Why have HR leadership at all if not to be the chief commitment officer and repository? Why else is HR there?

have the skill, experience, or courage to confront what's really going on. In any case, at times we find HR managers quite defensive and protective about the culture of their organization, mainly about the aspects that are not working. For the HR head who wants to address these issues, there is a clear and powerful framework in chapter 3.

Playing a bold leadership role in generating an environment of strategic commitment—that is, serving as a chief commitment officer—is, indeed, a challenge, and it is by no means simple. But the risk for HR executives of letting a culture of poor commitment perpetuate itself is far greater over time than the risk of offending the executive team. This is the role that anyone charged with nurturing an organization's "human resources" must play. And many HR leaders we have worked with have expressed passionately that this is the reason they became HR professionals in the first place, and it is, without compare, *the* most exciting part of their jobs. Monica Woods agrees: "I know that my ability to coach other leaders is directly tied to the degree of trust that exists between us, so I have made it a top priority to work on that, and in some cases it is challenging. However, I consider this the most important and exciting part of my job."

Another good example is John Powenski, head of the "People Team" within Capital One's system replacement effort (described at the beginning of Chapter 6). As the HR lead for this large and complex initiative he and his team played an instrumental role in creating a high performance environment for the project team to achieve outstanding results. In his own words Powenski says: "We knew our role was to partner with the project team in order to build strong commitment and accountability toward our aggressive strategy. Everything we did was geared toward that end."

"My team supported the leaders to monitor the commitment of the team. We developed an incentive program to help the leadership team reinforce desired behaviors, especially for delivering on commitments. Rather than a traditional morale survey, the metrics we used measured confidence in project leadership, cultural alignment, leadership behaviors and the support needed to deliver the business strategy. We monitored these vital signs on a quarterly basis, and met with Rob Alexander and his extended leadership team to help them address areas of concern immediately."

John and his team met regularly with work stream leaders to encourage and coach them to demonstrate appreciation for the personal sacrifices their team members were taking. Using incentives like handwritten thank you notes, gift cards, and spot bonuses, they helped leaders motivate associates to quickly address bottlenecks, escalate critical decisions, and illuminate workflow barriers. "The

People team was as much a part of the project as the developers, project managers and system architects; they were an integral part of our success," says Rob Alexander.

Stormy Weather:
The Role of Strategic Commitment in HR Transformation

In order for HR to generate an environment of strategic commitment throughout the organization, it needs to generate an environment of strategic commitment *within its own team!* HR has to be a role model and demonstrate the power of strategic commitment first.

This requires taking an honest, no-nonsense look at the current state of HR within the organization. It means telling the unvarnished truth about where internal customers are satisfied and where they are not, and where HR team members feel they are empowered and part of a difference-making, value-adding function and where they are not. And because HR is usually in the rear, not the vanguard, of strategic commitment (formally or informally), this is the most threatening but high-potential aspect of its transformation.

In a large service organization we worked with, the head of HR had a unique opportunity to make a difference because of his long-standing relationship with the CEO who trusted him completely. This HR executive—who really wanted to make a difference—focused his time and attention on trying to understand the issues in his business partner units. He launched numerous companywide initiatives to address what he believed were the key shortcomings of his stakeholders: leadership development and cultural improvement programs, to mention a couple. Unfortunately, he made some critical mistakes along the way.

He used his political capital with the CEO to get endorsements and mandates for programs he believed were best for the company, sometimes without recognizing the importance of getting real buy-in from his peer executives. Because the executives felt they had no

choice but to submit to what they believed were command decisions, they became resentful. This lack of peer buy-in resulted in
weak adoption of these efforts.

More important, his arrogance blinded him to the dysfunctional
dynamics within his own HR team. His campaigning for changes and
fixes to what he viewed as the biggest problems in the company as
a whole were met with increasing doubt, skepticism, and resistance
as his peers doubted his competence at demonstrating what he was
preaching within his own group. As a matter of fact, his HR group
was viewed as the worst off in some of the areas where he was pointing out the shortcomings of others.

His unwillingness to look inward and examine his own HR organization cost him his credibility, and thereby his ability to fulfill his
vision. Furthermore, his own team suffered as a result. Despite their
strong desire to partner with their internal customers, they found
themselves struggling with a negative HR reputation that undermined their ability to build strong individual partnerships and relationships. (Don't underestimate the power of negative perceptions.)
While this may be an extreme and unfortunate example, blindness
and lack of self-reflection within HR are not uncommon. If HR
truly wants to lead the way, it has to start with getting its own act
together.

HR can lead the change and add great value, *or* it can play a
passive role and merely follow the process (or, more probably, get
dragged along and trampled in the process). In the worst case, HR
can impede a change initiative by acting only as the guardian of
corporate resources and development initiatives. Under the banner
of "optimizing organizational talent and resources while maintaining
consistency," HR can stifle opportunities for innovation, collaboration, and breakthroughs in performance.

Unfortunately, the reason HR's reputation has lagged is because
for so long, in so many organizations, it has in fact been an inhibitor,

focused on its own agenda and self-preservation, out of touch with the issues that are really on people's minds.

As we have repeatedly trumpeted, it all starts with courage. If HR is not going to step up and lead change it should get out of the way. The CEO and the firm will be better off without HR if it insists on maintaining an antiquated view of its raison d'être.

CHAPTER 10

◆ ◆ ◆

STRATEGIC COMMITMENT AS ORGANIZATIONAL LIFESTYLE

Integrating the Process into Organizational DNA

Nothing can overcome the organizational immune system unless it has longevity. That means certain processes have to be inserted into the very fabric and life support system of the entity.

Strategic commitment is no different, and it therefore must become part of the respiratory system, if you will, of the corporate body.

You Get What You Pay For: Creating the Proper Reward System

Rewards and performance are linked (or should be), but higher rewards don't necessarily produce higher performance. Here are two instances:

□ Employees are most motivated by gratification in the work they do and recognition of that performance. (Motivation is intrinsic and self-generated, not introduced externally through pep talks and exercises like treading on hot coals.) If you give an unhappy employee more money, you simply have a wealthier unhappy employee. If I hate my working conditions, or the boss, or the customer interaction, more money doesn't change a whit of my nongratification with my circumstances.

◻ Sometimes rewards simply maintain the status quo. A few years ago, a consulting firm decided to offer a new Cadillac to the three field people securing the most new business. Guess what? The same three outstanding people who brought in the most business the year before did so again, without breaking a sweat. Except now the firm had over $100,000 less margin because it had to pay six figures to reward that which was completely unnecessary the previous year! Everyone else finished in the same order at the same levels of business.

Thus, rewards are much more than pay/compensation/monetary acknowledgment. That's too simple. But let's talk about pay first because, despite the fact that it is overrated as *the* source of performance, it is still a key influencer.

The bad news is that pay and performance do not have a one-for-one relationship; the good news is you can get significantly more than a 10 percent increase in performance *without having to pay people an additional 10 percent in wages*. In fact, you can get 20 percent, 30 percent, 40 percent, and more performance out of your employees. Higher pay does not *cause* better performance. But used in the right way, financial incentives can significantly enhance the degree to which people feel cared for.

> **StratComment**
> *You don't manage an organization through its compensation plan. You manage it through superb management. Strategic commitment is both an input and the output of that approach.*

While a proper reward system will not—in and of itself—cause people to shift from compliance to commitment, an inadequate or misguided reward system can easily erode people's desire to give their all.

When people are engaged and fulfilled, paying them more will make a difference. However, when they are bitter or dissatisfied (i.e., complying), paying them more will only make a small and insignificant difference (i.e., they'll be wealthier and still unhappy). Even though most executives/managers would agree with this statement, judging by actual behavior and actions it seems that most companies don't really get it. Most companies consider money as the first solution to any motivation issue.

Financial incentives also cannot substitute for perceptions regarding management credibility, courage, competence, and care.

For example, a friend of ours relayed a story of a botched merger in which many of the employees of the acquired company felt they were assessed unfairly and were slotted in roles and pay levels beneath that of their peers from the acquiring company. Without being transparent regarding the methods and criteria used for the assessments, management instituted a cost-saving initiative wherein the individual or team identifying a savings would be entitled to 5 percent of the total amount saved.

On paper, the program looked sound. However, the unaddressed negative sentiments from the job assessments and assignments sullied the environment to such a degree that employees had no desire to act in the best interests of the company. Most expressed this sentiment: "If the company doesn't really care about me, why should I do more than I have to just to get by?" The net result—very few cost savings were identified, making the initiative almost irrelevant.

We have seen situations time and again where ambitious, competent senior executives—whose generous compensation plans were based on mutual and collective success—failed to generate the open, honest, courageous, and collaborative interactions with their peers that would have allowed for the achievement of results needed for their maximum payouts. Despite their complete understanding of the financial prize available, they did not step up to the plate because of fear, politics, and self-protection, and they lost the bonus. The reason: Money doesn't make people courageous, sincere, collaborative, or effective. Commitment does.

While this book isn't about rewards, per se, we've found that the reward environment in many of our clients' companies has had to be drastically realigned in order to be consistent with strategic goals. Here is one of those examples that you just can't make up.

A major U.S. airline had embarked on a strategy of maximizing customer trust and dependence. The belief was that if fares were undifferentiated, consumers would choose the airline with the best responsiveness and transparency. In fact, it was thought that even if the airline's fares were slightly higher, potential flyers would still prefer the "caring carrier."

An ad campaign was prepared at the cost of several million dollars, and an equally impressive internal campaign for employees was launched, replete with wall plaques, meetings, and scripts. Phone agents in particular were encouraged to take the time to carefully tell customers about alternative routes and connections, and explain that some tickets might be less expensive if ordered on the website, and they were provided job aids with specific information about special charges for different services.

The tactics seemed totally in support of the strategy, right? Well, no, because middle management never stopped evaluating and rewarding agents on a certain key indicator. What was it? You've probably guessed: the number of callers handled per hour!

Here's another example on a more exalted level: We were involved with a Hewlett-Packard initiative that involved a more seamless client interface, with fewer different HP reps calling on the same large customers. Everyone was finally on board. But then, for the first time at a final meeting, the head of the printer operation appeared. At the time, this was the most profitable division at HP, and printer ink was the largest margin item in the entire company.

"We're not going along," the printer chief calmly announced, as though the Irish had once again defeated the Treaty of Lisbon for the

European Community. As the meeting quickly dissolved, someone asked him on the way out why he wouldn't go along.

"I'm focused on our division reaching or exceeding its goal. This initiative may be valuable for others, but it does nothing for me or my senior team," he said. In other words, here were outstanding performers unmoved by a plan that would bring no additional recognition or money for them.

Unfortunately, these two examples only begin to scratch the surface. There are many more corporate environments rife with compensation and rewards programs that run counter to stated organizational objectives. This topic is one of the most common areas of complaints we encounter. Some classics are sales programs that run counter to manufacturing, customer service, or quality initiatives; operations timelines and budgets that undermine sales initiatives; and on and on.

The Metrics of Commitment: Focusing on Output, Not Input

Are people focusing on the time they spend sweeping the floors, or on whether or not the floors are clean?

Too many organizations monitor activities, not progress and outcomes. Ask yourself:

- How many project meetings have been held?
- How many people are participating on cross-functional projects?
- How many people are responding to our surveys?
- How many customer focus groups have been conducted?
- How many suggestions have been submitted?

Remember when you were in grammar school? The teacher told you to stand up straight, maintain a straight line when walking as a group, keep quiet, keep your locker or workstation tidy, and so forth. Does walking in a straight line really prepare you for further learning and life's little competitive speed bumps? We think not.

Yet many modern organizations treat their employees as if they were in grammar school, focusing on arbitrary tasks and inputs, not on results and outputs.

A commitment without an outcome-oriented metric is meaningless. It's like measuring how many meetings started and ended on time, or whether the agenda items (i.e., times allotted to discuss each topic) were kept, rather than whether the objectives of the meeting were accomplished. (And, as no small matter, most meetings focus on inputs—things to discuss, items to process, bullet points to cross off—rather than ensuring actions, changes, and new outcomes.)

We always coach our clients to become oriented and focused on outcomes instead of activities. We encourage them to approach meetings the same way. Rather than the traditional meeting preparation process of gathering topics to discuss and assessing how long each discussion will take, we urge them to gather objectives—either prior to the meeting or at the outset—and then lead the discussion like this: "Here we are at the end of the meeting, and the meeting was successful. What three or four results did we achieve?" This way you are asking the group to be clear about the three or four outcomes to be realized. Then you orient the discussion around achieving each outcome. By aligning on outcomes, the team can manage the course and avoid setting off on tangents and getting off target. Most of our clients have reported that as a result, their meetings are shorter and much more productive—no small achievement in and of itself.

Here is an exercise that we propose for anyone having difficulty with this concept:

1. Choose at least three people you are responsible for managing and evaluating.

2. Read the documentation you've all agreed upon to measure

progress and success in terms of their contributions. (You have such documentation, right?)

3. Review the informal discussions you've had with them about progress and success (or lack thereof).

4. Assess whether the preponderance of these communications has been about results or activities. By preponderance, we mean better than 85 percent.

By using this exercise and participating in company meetings and evaluations, we have observed that there is a tropism that draws people to discuss and measure activity (in consulting, it's called "deliverables"). The default position is to talk about "how" and not "what."

We see this kind of thinking—and the resultant misguided behavior—every day. The car salesperson takes his turn and greets the next customer promptly, but is he pursuing the potential buyer's needs or merely spouting statistics about engine displacement and warranties? The server at the restaurant announces, "I'm Amanda and I'm your server," and takes the order without writing it down. But is the service attentive, friendly, and accurate? The organization returns the customer call or the e-mail inquiry, but is the customer satisfied and taken care of? Sales management assesses how many sales calls are made, but are they being made on the right prospects, conducted well, and—conceptual breakthrough—resulting in business?

We have been in scores of organizations where the entity had a mediocre year, but the majority of employees were rated *"exceeded expectations."* Now, how can that be?

We'll tell you how: The organization is judged (by the market, shareholders, and analysts) by its results, such as return on equity, return on investment, outcomes versus projections, and so forth. But the great majority of the employees were evaluated on *inputs*, such as getting to work on time,

> **StratComment**
>
> *Please don't explain why your system for winning at roulette is based on sophisticated algorithms and calculations. Show me your net winnings.*

dressing correctly, answering phones promptly, making service calls, producing reports, and providing forecasts and financial information (which are often wrong and never assessed from the standpoint of long-term accuracy, just as most prognosticators in the market or touts at the racetrack are not judged on eventual accuracy).

Picking and Choosing: How to Hire Talent That Thrives on Commitment

Someone said to us recently, "I had a good day today—no one asked me to do anything." Another time we invited people to describe what they most enjoyed about their work during a meeting we were conducting. In response, one woman said, "I consider work to be my eight-hour-a-day inconvenience."

Walking through a division with a Merck executive some years ago, we asked how things were going. "Not so good since Joe retired," he admitted.

"But Joe is right over there at his desk," we noted.

"Yes, I didn't say he had left, but he did retire."

Some people thrive on accomplishment, while others come to work for a paycheck. Your recruiting practices must be designed to weed out the caretakers from those who will commit to, own, and deliver on bold objectives.

It is not enough to screen people for technical and professional competence. There are plenty of highly skilled individuals who are loathe to take a risk or put themselves at stake for anything other than the accuracy of their work—and for some people that would be a stretch objective. Contrast that with someone who will commit to satisfying a customer, or galvanizing a team, or delivering on a sales quota. Those are the kind of people who will take the organization to the next level.

Here's the profile of an employee who has a strategic commitment orientation (as compared with a compliance-based employee):

Commitment

- Proactively suggests improvements
- Works longer hours on his own volition
- Pushes back on ideas deemed weak
- Takes pride in her own achievement
- Identifies with outputs of the work
- Prudent risk taker who will accept failure
- Informal leader
- Volunteers
- May be unpopular at times, and doesn't care
- Searches for cause

Compliance

- Only reacts to others' suggestions
- Works only by the clock
- Blames others when ideas fail
- Looks only to compensation
- Identifies with job title or position
- Conservative and risk-averse
- Permanent follower
- Passively accepts
- Seeks acceptance above all else
- Searches for blame

What kind of employees do you have working for you?

While we're at it, here is another way we discriminate among employees: skills versus will. Most people would agree that skills are teachable and come from a mix of knowledge and experience. So we can teach someone how to run a meeting, or find new prospects, or make the power plant more efficient. We know what has to be done and we've had experience doing it. Think of a ski instructor who knows how to teach you to bend your knees and lean into a turn, and has the experience of racing down all those black diamonds.

On the other hand, most people believe that will is more innate, like a talent one is either born with or not. However, we suggest that's not the case; rather, we believe that will *can* be developed, improved, and cultivated. We've seen many command-and-control leaders, people who might have been called uncaring or arrogant, metamorphose and become much more collaborative, empathic, and open. No, their DNA did not change, and in comparison to other beacons they may still fall short. However, the will they generated enabled them to dramatically improve themselves as leaders in these areas, as recognized by others around them.

In contrast, there are also those with great skills and even talent who, due to a lack of will, become stagnant, cynical, and resigned. Take, for example, playing the piano, or singing, or playing a sport. Skills training can make the horrible bearable, but never excellent. Will is required. (How many times have you heard a bored, alienated employee ritually repeat the words "Have a nice day," but with an inflection that indicates she actually hopes that you get hit by a car?) Our resigned, cynical "54-months-to-go" fellow, who we mentioned in chapter 1, may well have been an expert in his field, but his contribution to his team was doubtful given his lack of will. The most vital kind of business talent is will—desire, enthusiasm, passion, energy, and self-motivation. The rule, therefore, is to hire for will and teach the skills, not the other way around.

Understand also that a stress-free environment is not a committed environment. Take a look at the bell curve in Figure 10-1.

As you can see, low stress creates low productivity and a perception of entitlement. (Joe is still here, but he's "retired.") At the lower numbers, the attitude is, "I'm not doing anything much, you're lucky I'm here today." But high stress also creates low productivity because people are paralyzed. This is a fear mentality. ("If they can't find me, they can't hurt me. I'm keeping my head low.")

Only in the middle condition—moderate stress—do you create an environment of pride. This is where the adrenaline is flowing, there is a healthy sense of urgency, and people are innovative and risk taking. Deadlines may loom, but don't worry, we'll make it. You want your people, ideally, at 6.5 on our chart.

High-commitment employees are at home in conditions of moderate stress. The opposite of distress is eustress.

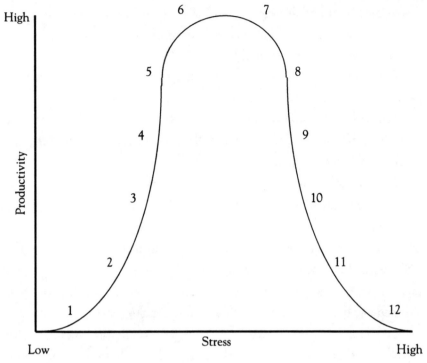

Figure 10-1. Productivity and stress.

Communicating Commitment:
Changing the Nature of Feedback

Organizations that embrace the notion of strategic commitment evaluate themselves on at least two dimensions: Are the results be-ing achieved (i.e., is there an environment of accountability where people are making and keeping promises)? And are people engaged and fostering an environment for others to be engaged (i.e., are people operating as business owners with a high level of personal responsibility rather than with a victim mentality where it's always someone else's fault)?

GE uses a "Results and Living the Values" matrix. Capital One uses an "Excellence/Do the Right Thing" matrix, which they refer-ence on their website. Tony Marano of Lucent had a sign on his desk that he looked at near the end of each day that asked, "Are the results being delivered? Are my people ignited?" It was, he says, the key to being an "inspirational leader."

If managers are achieving the desired results but at the cost of people's attitudes, morale, and commitment, then they may discover that although this quarter may be fine, the numbers will eventually catch up and future performance will suffer. Under Jack Welch, GE found that achieving corporate objectives *in the wrong manner* was no better than not achieving corporate objectives. Once GE fired a few people over that, the message became quite clear.

In most companies, despite all the corporate slogans, there isn't a culture of feedback and honest communication. Frequently, 360-degree feedback processes are used to assess and support managers, but the feedback-givers remain anonymous and the process is focused on gathering content and data. At the end, a summary is produced and the manager being assessed gets a report with the findings but not who said what. While the process is beneficial, it misses a big opportunity—that is, the opportunity of having feedback as a natural and regular expression of open, honest, and productive communication. This environment of communication doesn't require people being anonymous or in hiding. In a strategic commitment environment, open, honest, authentic, blunt, and even courageous communication and feedback are values and a core foundation.

Let's be very clear about that last point. We take issue with the efficacy of 360-degree feedback instruments because their very intent (i.e., their stated value) is often to preserve anonymity. That, to us, is the sign of an unhealthy and uncommitted environment. It means that we are risk-averse, not proactive, and not personally engaged in outcomes. If we can't openly discuss our performance with each other—with our superiors, subordinates, peers, or simply colleagues—then how committed are we to mutual success? Or, to put it another way, how strong is commitment in opposition to politics, cliques, and fear?

There is as much, if not more, value in people getting feedback as in giving it, in real time, while looking in the eye of the person providing the feedback. Communication has two dimensions to it: the content it delivers and transfers, and the experience it generates. Tone of voice, body language, what gets conveyed by looking in each other's eyes or listening to someone's voice are all a part of that experience. Many organizations are global, so people are not working in the same office. We are not saying that people need to be talking in person. Phone, video, and even e-mails sometimes can still be enough to maintain the personal, open, honest communication quality. And there is great work being done on "virtual" offices and meetings so that we can interact on a quality basis even from different continents.

"The feedback we gave each other around our leadership strengths and weaknesses was invaluable," says Scott Gaul, VP of Financial Planning and Analysis within Prudential's Retirement Business Unit. "And the fact that it was face-to-face made it especially useful. I had heard some of those same comments before, but they never meant as much and I never understood them so well. It also improved my group's ability to be direct and straight with each other about process issues that need fixing."

Jim Burns and his team at a global telecommunications company, along with hundreds of other groups we've worked with, expressed very similar sentiments. In one of Burns's meetings with his senior team, he asked everyone to write down two areas of leadership strength and two areas of weakness for themselves, as well as for each of their peers around the table. The room was silent for about twenty minutes as people were writing their observations and assessments.

When everybody was done he had each person share the self-assessment, and then everyone around the table gave that person direct feedback as well. Rather than the anonymous 360-degree surveys where people get feedback but often don't know who said what,

Burns chose to collect feedback in an open, honest manner, and he included himself.

"People were a bit hesitant at first, but by the second and third rounds of feedback they felt the environment was safe and supportive, and the feedback and coaching comments became extremely blunt and powerful," said Peter McNally, Burns's HR director. When it came time for Burns's feedback, there were two prevalent messages: Almost everyone expressed their positive feelings that he served as a role model because he lived up to his own extraordinarily high standards. At the same time, however, these same high standards left people feeling frustrated, because they did not feel they could live up to them.

"Jim's recognition of this issue, and his subsequent commitment to meet with each of his reports to align on how best to match his standards and their individual management styles, was a clear demonstration of his commitment to lead by example. That's how he's made the U.K. division as successful as it is," added McNally.

> **StratComment**
>
> *No one believes, in organizational life, what they read or what they are told. They only believe what they see and experience.*

Feedback around commitment needs to be just as blunt as feedback around results. If managers know they can "beat the system" by producing results through manipulation, coercion, or some other manner of being disingenuous, many of them will. And almost everyone around will eventually emulate this behavior if it is rewarded!

Figure 10-2 is a list of questions managers can ask when making assessments and providing feedback to employees. These questions should capture the spirit, character, style, behaviors, effort, actions and outcomes of the person being assessed, while taking into account the individual's position in the company.

The very nature of organizational feedback needs changing in any case, and certainly for strategic commitment to flourish. (And

Figure 10-2. Strengths and weaknesses assessment criteria:

Do they orient themselves around making a difference, rather than protecting their own ego and status?

- Are they focused on empowering others and making a difference, rather than on their own interests and self-promotion?
- Are they interested and fully invested in making others around them great (e.g., making others stars or successful)?
- Do they identify their own success with the success of their people, rather than their own personal agenda?

Do they make the organization's vision come alive in a meaningful way?

- Are they clear about our vision?
- Do they deal with large and small issues from the bigger picture of what is best for the whole organization, not merely for me or my area?
- Do they reference our vision in meetings and discussions?
- Do they present our vision effectively?

Are they authentic in all behaviors and communications?

- Are they real, genuine, vulnerable, and sincere?
- Do they operate with no hidden agendas?
- Are they transparent about motives and intentions?

Do they operate with integrity?

- Are they reliable and credible?
- Are they clear about commitments they make no matter how big or small, and do they consistently deliver on those commitments, without excuses?

Do they act and behave with boldness and courage?

- Do they take risks, challenge the status quo, and make bold decisions rather than adapt, conform to, or tolerate undermining or counterproductive behaviors or conversations?
- Do they operate with a winning, "unstoppable," and "uncircumstantial" (i.e., no excuses) spirit?

(continued)

Figure 10-2. Strengths and weaknesses assessment criteria: (continued)

Do they have other's backs unconditionally?

- Do they collaborate, cooperate, care, and team effectively?
- Are they "for each other," and do they operate from the premise of being "one team"?

Do they communicate openly and honestly?

- Do they talk straight to anyone at all levels and across all functions, no matter how uncomfortable it may be, without withholding or avoiding difficult conversations?

Do they generate passion, energy, and enthusiasm everywhere?

- Are they constantly energizing, motivating, and rallying people to work together around a common cause, creating a sense of fun and energy even around the mundane and serious work?
- Are they inspiring others to be passionate?

Do they build and empower leaders around them?

- Do they passionately promote leadership?
- Are they passionately committed to mentoring, coaching, and empowering leaders everywhere?
- Do they constantly demand people around them step up from a leadership standpoint, and relate to challenges as opportunities to elevate leadership?
- Do they demonstrate the same in their own behavior?

Are they committed to development and growth?

- Do they demonstrate commitment to their own personal development and growth?
- Do they promote the development and growth of others?
- Are they completely open to, not defensive or pretentious about, coaching and feedback, especially about areas of weakness?

remember our cause/effect dynamic, in that effective strategic commitment will then engender more open and honest feedback.) Here are some principles and practices for more powerfully and effectively engaging in the giving and receiving of feedback:

- *Formal evaluations should be performed conversationally on a monthly basis at the least, with formal, documented evaluations quarterly.* At year-end, no one should be surprised one iota about his or her performance evaluation, because it has been an ongoing process, not an event.

- *Meetings should never be held to merely share or distribute information, which is better done through e-mail or reports.* Meetings should only be held to generate results that are best achieved through bright people exchanging ideas interactively.

- *Feedback should always be attributed to a person or group.* Combining observed behavior and/or evidence with people's sentiments and perceptions can be very powerful, since both have merit. "They are saying . . ." or "I heard the other day . . ." are useful comments in the context of perception being reality. When you say, "I saw you do this . . ." the feedback becomes that much more real and tangible.

- *Feedback should be an organizational habit, not an event.* It should not be determined by a schedule but rather by the day-to-day need of team members to continuously support, elevate, coach, and correct each other.

- *Feedback is about making a difference, not about unloading everything on one's mind.* While one might have a strongly held opinion or feeling about another individual or group, the orientation that will be the most useful is to ask,

StratComment

"Getting it off my chest" may release one's angst, but it will make no difference.

"How can this make the biggest difference?" The aim is balancing the need for direct, blunt, and complete expression while ensuring that the receiver can hear it, own it, and ultimately be strengthened by it—even when the content of the message may be tough and/or uncomfortable.

- *When receiving feedback, you should listen as a partner, rather than as a lawyer.* Listen not just to what is being said, but to where the person is coming from. Don't scrutinize the accuracy of the words; rather, try to get the fullness of their perspective and concerns. Trust that they have your best interests in mind. As we often tell people, "Open both your ears and your heart to the feedback."

You must walk the talk and talk the walk. Top management exemplifies the behaviors that are desired in terms of rewards and feedback, and it must also talk about why the behaviors are making a difference. For more guidelines on giving and receiving feedback, see Appendix.

Choosing Your Friends:
Alliances, Vendors, and Contractors in the Fold

Once you have created an environment of strategic commitment inside your organization, the opportunity arises to expand to all internal and external partners. (We have found with most of our clients that it becomes a matter of value and principle to do so after awhile.)

This idea is hardly groundbreaking. The quality movements among major manufacturers quickly spread to their suppliers and some customers as a means of exponentially expanding the power of the approaches. (And in several instances it was a way of ensuring that the vendors still had preferred status with their customer!)

Most traditional relationships with vendors and contractors can be described as "vendor/supplier relationships." They are based on fulfilling requests as reliably as possible, trying not to screw up (at least not publicly), and making as much money from the sales of your products as possible. Trust doesn't have to be very high, and as long as the supplier provides the goods in a reliable and acceptable way, everyone is happy.

> **StratComment**
>
> *It's tough to speak Latin well if you return to a Greek-speaking world, and it's tough to fully realize the benefits of strategic commitment if your key business partners and relationships are not involved in it.*

In an environment of strategic commitment, this relationship is often insufficient, so the opportunity and need to elevate it to a relationship based on being a "business partner" is compelling.

This is not merely a cosmetic change, it is a significant one because it involves:

- Listening to and anticipating the needs of your customer, and making offers consistent with what you believe they now (or will in the future) need to help their business.

- Immediately and thoroughly addressing breakdowns in performance by taking responsibility for any negative impact on the customer, demonstrating a commitment to the partner by correcting the source of the breakdown, and actually correcting the problem so there is no recurrence. In this way, breakdowns can actually serve to strengthen the partnership.

- Collaborating on ways to improve the overall benefits to both parties on an ongoing basis.

- Suggesting new ideas that will require substantial changes in your own operation because they are for the long-term good of the partnership (and, therefore, your own business)— and that includes changes that might cause you to sacrifice short-term results.

- Making investments in projects, initiatives, and R & D based on mutually beneficial objectives for the sake of deepening and cementing the long-term partnership.

- Involving disparate parties who are not often involved in design or "upstream" work and strategy. Including a vanity mirror on the driver's side of the car is the argument for allowing half of your buying audience to participate in fundamental design.

- Having the confidence to share initiatives and strategies, with the knowledge that you may be told, justifiably, that you are wrong and you'll have to change your mind, or you'll be told, unjustifiably, that you are wrong, and you'll have to change some other minds.

- Ending relationships, internally and externally, because the other party simply cannot buy in to the idea. In effect, you may fail to gain strategic commitment, and in these cases parting ways beats lowering your standards.

- Engaging in what the psychologists term "meta-talk," meaning that you will not only deal honestly about issues facing you via frank communication, honest feedback, and accurate incentive, but you'll also talk candidly *about* the communication, feedback, and incentive. You don't just enjoy the relationship, you talk about the relationship with the intent of keeping it fresh, vibrant, and improving.

- Enabling and empowering subordinates to challenge their superiors when issues around customer feedback, evaluation, and satisfaction need attention. This can be a growth experience or a threatening experience for senior management.

- Internalizing the belief that changing your behavior in response to solicited or unsolicited feedback from business partners (those who are mutually engaged in strategic commitment) is the rule, not the exception. It is healthy behavior, not unhealthy, and it is the route to a better future.

We have tried to demonstrate in this chapter that you don't adopt or adapt to strategic commitment; rather, it needs to become part of the organization's lifeblood, its DNA, its life support system. When done well, strategic commitment thus creates a virtuous circle of increased desire and momentum for positive change, which fuels self-sustaining, continuous growth.

Now, we'll take a deeper look at the diversity applicable for strategic commitment and delve into some very particular types of organizations and needs.

CHAPTER 11

♦ ♦ ♦

THE DIVERSITY OF STRATEGIC COMMITMENT

There Is No Such Thing as "But We're Different"

If strategic commitment is legitimate and worthwhile, then it should be relevant and applicable in virtually any environment, regardless of the sector or culture. That's not an easy position to which to aspire, and it's why we didn't write this book ten years ago. But with hundreds of clients in seventy countries in both for-profit and nonprofit markets, we can now make that conclusion.

Since we expect our readership to be as diverse as our client base, we are devoting this chapter to the pragmatic application in such environments, including government, education, start-ups, and other traditional "backwaters" of modern and aggressive organization development.

Never fear, you are not that different, as fond as you may be of saying that.

Nonprofits Are Not a Synonym for "Unprofessional"

Many not-for-profit organizations, be they community-oriented (e.g., the United Way, Rotary Clubs, shelters of various kinds), religious in nature (churches, synagogues, mosques, or other nonsecular establishments), or cause-related (e.g., American Cancer Society, UNICEF, or the Red Cross), have organizational structures and managerial competence paralleling that of the private sector. In fact, a good many of these organizations have executives who once ran (or may well run in the future) large for-profit organizations. They are also very often governed by boards filled with professional, experienced executives from the for-profit world.

Peter Drucker once famously remarked that he thought the Girl Scouts was the best-run organization of any kind, public or private, in the United States. At the same time, the Boy Scouts became involved in bitter internal dissention and public relations nightmares. This is not different from Enterprise Rent-a-Car having a good year while Hertz is down.

There are some significant differences between the for- and not-for-profit work environments, including compensation, governance, and legal and stakeholder structures, to mention a few. However, nonprofits have the same need for strategic commitment as for-profits do.

> **StratComment**
> *Please don't hide behind the "we're different" rubric. Every organization is somewhat different but, like people around the world, most organizations are far more similar than dissimilar.*

- Although they are called nonprofits, on an operating basis (day-to-day) they are run exactly the same as for-profits. They have a chief executive, staff, budgets, capital expenditures, and monthly and quarterly reporting cycles—all of which puts the same pressures on them to deliver results, just like for-profits.

- Politics in the nonprofit world are often quite thorny. Board memberships can be seen as résumé icing or trophies for sale to the highest bidder (by way of donation size), so the size of one's pocketbook trumps the power of good ideas and good deeds. Board members are typically long-tenured and filled with old-fashioned ideas and ways of doing things. When new board members are elected (which is infrequent), tensions between the old and new are common.

◻ In the nonprofit world, executives are often overly concerned with pleasing board members to push their own priorities and decisions through. As a result, these executives are perceived by their own staffs as basing their decisions and leadership on politics rather than sincere, courageous, competent, and caring choices.

◻ Paid nonprofit staff members often feel unappreciated for their efforts, yet they do not want to bite the hand that feeds them by pointing out shortcomings in board members' time, effort, or financial contributions. There can be significant tensions and suspicions among board members, paid staff, part-time staff, and volunteers.

◻ Nonprofits are funded by donations and feel a high degree of fiduciary responsibility and scrutiny regarding where and how to spend those always-precious funds to make the greatest impact, and the number of people who have a vote about where those funds get spent is significantly greater than the for-profits.

◻ Much of the workforce is made up of volunteers who have different motives and perspectives, yet in many ways are no different from employees in traditional organizations—*except that they have more of a natural passion for the cause!*

Given all of the above—and more—the need for generating an environment of strategic commitment in which all staff, board members, and volunteers are truly on the same page with a shared vision and set of commitments is as great, if not greater, than in the corporate world.

Rules for Gaining Strategic Commitment in Nonprofits

Here, then, are our rules and guidelines for gaining strategic commitment in nonprofits. These recommendations may apply to other categories of organizations as well, including educational, government, and volunteer organizations (each of which is also discussed in this chapter), so consider these essential rules no matter what type of institution you are leading.

1. *Make strategic commitment a key emphasis area for the executive director* (or whoever the top staff member may be) and evaluate this individual on progress during the year. Just as in for-profits, the board (and especially the chair) should not micromanage the process. It is up to the chief executive officer to be the avatar, supporter, and evaluator of strategic commitment and demonstrate to the board that it is being managed properly.

2. *Address the content and context drivers of the strategy with the staff and key volunteers.* Have them be an integral part of creating a bold and compelling future for the organization, and then take ownership for the key areas of execution.

3. *Once the bold, compelling future has been crafted by the staff and select volunteers, continue to expand the platform of strategic commitment throughout the entire volunteer community.* It is critical that the chief executive inspire and fully engage this constituency. While there are always concerns about encroaching on the volunteer's time, it has been our experience that volunteers are usually as available as the mission of the organization inspires them to be. Lack of participation from this group is less a function of calendars than of their sense of feeling connected to what is being created, including their attraction to the sincerity, courage, competence and care of the leader. We were invited by a New York area United Way office to support them in their strategic planning process. They were facing an environment of consistently

decreasing funding and increasing competition for donations, which required them to elevate their brand to attract a broader donor base. Rather than doing it in the traditional way, which was to have a committee put together a binder that nobody would read, we pushed for an offsite meeting with the entire staff and a significant portion of the volunteer board. The CEO was intrigued and excited about the idea, yet also skeptical about his ability to get volunteers to commit to the one and a half days of personal time (over a weekend, no less) required for this effort. "It's so hard to get these people to come to our monthly two-hour board meetings," he said.

With lots of preparation we were able to persuade almost everyone who was invited to attend, and the meeting was a raving success. Everyone walked out aligned on a bold future they had created, excited about working together to make it happen. In fact, the buzz they created was so strong that the board members who had not been able to attend the offsite event insisted on convening a special meeting just so they could be included.

4. *Invite staff to some board meetings.* It is critical that staff and board members have an opportunity to stare each other in the eye and realize that neither group is out to undermine or embarrass the other.

5. *Create a rational board size.* Typically, this is no more than two dozen people. If politics or regional representation demand more board members, then operate through an executive committee of a dozen to two dozen members. You will have much more difficulty gaining strategic commitment in a loud crowd where interests collide.

We can make a case that strategic commitment is even *more* important for nonprofits, in consideration of their looser control over key resources (e.g., unearned income, volunteers) and often highly politicized boards whose members have quite divergent interests. We have successfully introduced this concept into battered women's shelters, arts groups of all kinds, community impact groups, charities, and many others.

Educational Institutions Need to Learn Something

The academic world, while honorable in intent and charged with the responsibility of helping to shape future leaders of social, economic, and political institutions, is unfortunately home to incredibly unhealthy politics and interactions among its members. (We are tempted to say, "Don't get us started!")

Competition for tenure and positions of authority is fierce. Challenge a colleague in the wrong forum or in ways that undermine credibility today—even if the merits of the challenge are valid—and one can pay for years to come. We have heard stories of medical papers outlining breakthrough procedures that were left unread and unpublished out of spite because of decades-old grievances by credit-grabbing professors in the medical community.

Yet things are changing. In fact, we can make the case that this is the best time of all to introduce strategic commitment to the academic/educational world because the older "baby boomer" professors are reaching retirement age. They are basically the more activist, liberal, and combative of all faculty members (by their own admission). They are being replaced by a younger cohort of PhDs who are much less influenced by the college turbulence of the 1960s (events that happened well before they were born) and much more interested in securing positions that feed both their intellectual needs and their families.

Moreover, aggressive university diversity initiatives have further changed the campus climate and created highly varied new faculties, including many immigrants and foreign professors on loan. Thus:

- Politics and unhealthy competition between colleagues in the teacher's lounge, once pervasive, are being replaced with a new sense of community and competition with other institutions, replacing internecine warfare.

◻ In spite of the noble aim of most universities, donations from alumni and grants from an assortment of sources are more important than ever, especially in tough economic times. Hence, more and more cooperation is required to outperform the competition in appealing to these sources.

◻ Contrary to naive notions that educational institutions are run as "one big happy family," they are run like businesses with hierarchies, budgets, and management structures. They need to create the same efficiencies and effectiveness that the private sector requires for strength. You can no more tolerate the history and anthropology departments fighting publicly than Toyota can afford its R & D and marketing functions to engage in public squabbles.

Here's another sign of the times in this regard: For the first time in a decade, Stanford University's anthropology department has reunited after a bitter schism had divided them into the biologists and the "bone people." The new generation of professors wants none of that.

> **StratComment**
>
> *The process needs of organizations—effectiveness, competitiveness, innovation, public relations, and so on—outweigh differences in the profit motive and points of origin.*

With all of this change on campus a growing reality, we urge leaders in the academic and educational communities to institute strategic commitment.

Governmental Agencies Can Actually Achieve Operating Efficiencies

Nothing we have ever experienced in seventy countries and working with hundreds of clients (with the possible exception of root canal without anesthesia) meets with less enthusiasm than getting one's motor vehicle license renewed in the United States. As a close second, a trip to the post office is as far from a racecar pit stop as can be imagined. But this does not have to be the case. Really.

Let's take a look at strategic commitment in government and in its fuel source, politics.

In the United States, as in most countries of the industrialized world and many other parts of the world as well, the president, prime minister, or equivalent is also nominally the chief executive of that country. In that capacity, the context drivers shaping strategic commitment have everything to do with this person's ability to effectively lead that country.

Without commenting on the pros or cons of undertaking the second war in Iraq, George W. Bush suffered greatly in public opinion because of perceptions of a lack of transparency in the way his administration engaged in "selling" the initial invasion to the American public. He subsequently received the lowest approval ratings ever for a sitting president.

While popularity should never be the key aim of an elected official, the lesson here is that the factors driving employees to embrace and take ownership for an organization's strategic direction—perceptions about their leaders' sincerity, courage, competence, and care, manifested in the political world in sound principles and policies and doing what's right for the constituents—are in fact the ingredients shaping people's choices regarding who they want to lead

StratComment
Whenever politicians say, "What the people of this country want," they are trying to create an assumptive strategic commitment. The problem is that the assumption is too often self-serving, and people readily proclaim, "But that's not what I want!"

their country. Despite the conventional wisdom that politicians will say and do anything to get elected, it certainly appeared that in the 2008 national election in the United States, people more than ever screened potential office holders based on these criteria.

Let's examine four aspects of government and politics that beg for strategic commitment at all levels:

1. *The massive amounts of volunteers needed for political campaigns at the grass-roots levels are far better handled within the framework of strategic commitment.* Many Barack Obama supporters became disenchanted when they thought their candidate had changed his stance on withdrawing troops from Iraq, for example. The old-style notion of "staying on message," when that message is designed in a backroom with campaign operatives, no longer has power with potential supporters who are evaluating every shrug and moan online at blogs, LinkedIn, Twitter, Facebook, YouTube, and so forth.

2. *Municipal functions—planning boards, school boards, zoning boards, fire districts, and so on—can no longer afford an "us against them" mentality with the citizenry whose taxes are instrumental for virtually all local initiatives.* This is especially true in the era of declining federal and state support. As an example, as chair of the East Greenwich, Rhode Island, planning board, Alan Weiss organized citizen committees of merchants, local officials, and consumers to recommend changes in traffic circulation, environmental aesthetics, and marketing of the city. These initiatives could be confidently acted on by the town council because of the broad band of support. But imagine these issues being simply imposed by the government? Immediate skepticism would doom even the most reasonable measure, or at least seriously delay it.

3. *Current trends toward nongovernment support in many areas will free up scarce funds and resources for true government responsibilities, such as infrastructure and safety.* Faith-based and citizen-supported community help, for example, requires strategic commitment and buy-in that the government must do things that only it can do, but not things that others can do as well or even better. (Don't laugh. The postal service is already a quasi-private agency, and it will probably become completely privatized down the road since FedEx already

carries the preponderance of U.S. mail on long-distance routes. Did you ever think you'd see that?)

4. *It is becoming apparent that the traditional source of school funding—property taxes—is no longer either sufficient or fair in terms of providing adequate education (of the government-subsidized type) throughout a state.* Strategic commitment has already provided the cohesion for communities to form charter schools, which would have once been unthinkable in the face of virulent opposition from the teachers union. Homeschooling has become an accepted part of the system, including participation in extracurricular events at local schools (and nowadays even some graduation ceremonies).

We don't find it shocking to suggest that strategic commitment will grow as a motive force in government and politics; in fact, we are surprised anyone would be stunned by that reality. Strategic commitment provides the interstitial "glue" to bring disparate groups and interests together under one "tent," thus allowing for an objective set of strategic goals (no matter what they may be called) to be supported by everyone.

Volunteer Organizations Require Strategic Commitment More Than Others

It might be that the goal of for-profit organizations is to create an environment where people behave as though they are volunteers. In other words, they are doing their jobs out of a commitment to do what is right for the good of the whole, rather than for a paycheck or for credit. At the same time, the dynamics of nonprofits, as described previously in this chapter, impede many volunteer organizations.

It becomes all the more important, then, to create a clear, compelling, and measurable outcome that inspires the people doing the work, while attracting sufficient funds to allow the organization to make as big an impact on its stated aim as possible.

Volunteer organizations have looser formal connections. By that we mean:

- *The board often meets in a perfunctory manner, with little common commitment or even understanding.* Example: A major volunteer organization was planning a strategy retreat. One board member, who represented a large for-profit with potential to contribute major support, said, "That's fine, but we're not going to have the time to take part in that initiative."

- *The quality of volunteerism is diverse, ranging from long-time acolytes to short-term interns.* There can easily be a "what's in it for me" mentality that supersedes the mission and goals of the organization and its outreach.

- *A relatively small staff is wearing a multitude of hats, doing many things adequately but few things really well.* Consequently, there is a constant "fire drill" atmosphere where chaos rules. Example: In working with a largely volunteer arts group, we found that the executive director and the organization were actually codependent. The executive directory was lax and distracted, causing the board to constantly extend deadlines or require additional money. In turn, the board's actions enabled the executive director to continue being lax and late. It was a vicious cycle.

- *A "poverty mentality" often develops, whereby the staff and board accept and overlook poor quality and slow responsiveness because they "can't afford anything better."* This results in mutual commiseration and false bravado about "what we've achieved with so little," instead of honest analysis about what really needs to be done.

> **StratComment**
> *Volunteer organizations need the social cohesion of strategic commitment more than any other kind of organization.*

◻ *Funding sources and community support ebbs and flows, so there are few long-term intricate relationships.* Or, where funding sources do exist, nonprofits are always sensitive to the fact that their disappearance could cause disaster. Example: In an arts group, $50,000 in promised sponsorship—about 10 percent of the budget—disappeared when the patron's suggestion for a performance was (justifiably) rejected because it did not meet the art group's quality standards.

◻ *Regimes change.* It would be laughable if it weren't so serious, and it is especially true with an increasing trend toward term limits of officers and members. A given chair or president has a "campaign" or "motto" or "crusade" that lasts for their tenure, usually a year or two at most. Then a new regime enters with a new mood and tenor. So the banners, stationery, and events are commensurately changed while, theoretically, the organization's mission grinds on. It's like a periodic tremor that shakes up the staff and volunteers (who *are* constant) and creates loose bricks and mortar.

◻ *Volunteer groups are held together and bound traditionally through passion, belief, and faith (in the cause, not necessarily religious faith, although that can also be a factor).* Therefore, the seeds of strategic commitment are sown, but too often that passion is not controlled and targeted. Example: We have coached people consulting with church groups where the internecine warfare was worse than anything you'd see in a high-powered investment firm, and where rivals were actually splitting up the congregation, including dueling ministers.

◻ *Volunteer organizations come and go.* Their cause or mission might have been met or superseded. They might have been together for a transient need (e.g., raising building funds). They may be embraced by a larger entity. Because of those dynamics, it's important to use strategic commitment to develop quick and effective cohesion in as little time as possible. No one in this area can afford to use up precious time, credibility, resources, money, and volunteers on miscommunication, unshared goals, confusion, and/or lethargy.

The basics of the process—involvement, feedback, identification with a common cause, the belief that one is an "owner" of the enterprise, and so forth—are vital to the success of all types of volunteer organizations, whether the intricate and global Rotary Clubs or the local Little League or Parent-Teacher Association. Our observation is that the willingness and intent to "do good" is not enough. There must also be a framework and belief system within which one *can* do good.

Start-Ups: Strategic Commitment in the Petri Dish

We have found that young companies can have old mind-sets!

Unencumbered by bureaucracy and the handcuffs of big-company rules, regulations, and committees, start-ups may seem a place where strategic commitment grows naturally. And, in fact, that sometimes is the case. However, there are too many exceptions to this logic.

We once worked with a well-known commercial artist who was committed to significantly expanding his revenues. While his entire staff of fifteen people enjoyed a relaxed, friendly, "we all love each other" work environment, the lack of clarity around roles and responsibilities, and around holding each other to account for deadlines and commitments, created an enormous undercurrent of frustration and resentment. So while the need in large organizations is often for increased autonomy and innovation, entrepreneurial shops can build strategic commitment by *increasing* structure and discipline! That sounds counterintuitive, but it makes eminent sense.

They must also simultaneously employ the principles of open, honest, and candid communication—a broken commitment in an entrepreneurial shop creates the same distrust as in the most bureaucratic of environments. As a matter of fact, the politics can increase in direct proportion to the rapid growth of these organizations. It is critical that leaders of these organizations do not consider themselves immune from the same toxic politics and counterproductive behaviors they often left behind when they fled to start their own endeavor. In fact, some are "carriers" for the behaviors they viewed as undesirable, which makes them complacent and/or blind to the source of potential commitment problems.

At a small high-tech start-up we worked with, the CEO shared the following story. He walked into the break area one morning and encountered a new hire (from a nearby large manufacturing company) with a petition full of signatures. When the CEO inquired as to the cause, the employee said he was gathering support for a wider selection of refreshments to be made available in the coffee room. Stunned, the CEO tore the petition in half and told the new hire to simply go ask the office manager for what he and his coworkers wanted.

Most of us in entrepreneurial activities are refugees from large firms. That "exodus" makes us even better at our new ventures. (We're using the first-person plural because the three of us fit that profile perfectly.) We know what stifled us and our colleagues; we are all too familiar with the toxicity of corporate politics; we have firsthand evidence of the half-life of poor hires and appointments; and we have some idea of the utopian village we'd prefer to create.

Then what goes wrong with start-ups, fueled as they are by passion and those fleeing injustice? Think about this: How many people have successfully started new ventures but turned out to be precisely the wrong people to run them on a longer-term basis? Steve Jobs and Apple, Inc. are exceptions, although even he went on a long hiatus from the organization.

Instead, here's what we tend to see:

◻ The once-revered founder becomes the butt of jokes or attracts the scorn of a "younger set." (This was a problem at Polaroid as Edwin Land became increasingly frustrated trying to make his once-innovative business successful.)

◻ Decisions are made on the basis of "old retainers" and not market reality or leading-edge intent. (After all, "They were here with me at the outset and shouldered the risk.")

◻ An ironic conservatism enters the equation once the lawyers and accountants come on board. They are suddenly claiming that things have to "slow down," or once-important risk taking is "no longer prudent," or "we'll be in trouble with the IRS or industry regulators."

StratComment

Start-ups tend to "age" at a more rapid pace than traditional organizations if they are not managed and led well in terms of the very strengths they innately possess.

◻ Alternatively, a blind adherence to "what got us here" creates an atmosphere of continuing risk, acquisition, and seat-of-the-pants leadership. At best, this disorganized approach plateaus the organization through the creation of as many failures as victories when momentum means everything.

Thus, there are two extremes: an insidious conservatism and an imprudent haphazardness. Either is deadly. The antidote is strategic commitment as part of the start-up process.

We worked with an Internet advertising firm that had outstanding founding partners with terrific expertise. However, it became increasingly clear that the sales force couldn't simply proceed with quotas for new business on "click through" advertising. They, too, had to believe in the cause, in the passion of the place (providing economical advertising more effectively than traditional sources, from which all the founders originated). Then, we all realized, that the sales team wasn't enough, but that administrative people, technical people, and R & D needed to be included, too. That kind of strategic commitment in start-up organizations affords the following huge advantages:

1. *Strength and Courage*. These are qualities that are needed to get through inevitable down times. People can rally around a common and shared vision.

2. *Virtual Ownership in the Company to Parallel the Founders' Ownership*. Employees can be rewarded with phantom stock and other very real benefits.

3. *Greater Innovation*. The most powerful innovation originates with frontline people who deal with the project, service, and customer relationship every day.

4. *More Rapid Feedback About What Is Working and What Isn't*. IBM can afford $15 million errors and never stumble. A start-up can make a $15,000 error and fall on its face. Therefore, the agility and "flatness" of a start-up is enhanced with strategic commitment so that gains can be exploited rapidly and errors cauterized quickly.

5. *Greater Sacrifice*. We are always observing whether everyone clears out at 5:00 p.m. (or even 4:45 to "beat the traffic") or if most employees linger until 6:00 p.m., with some phones still being answered. Will people work overtime and will they come in on weekends? Do they "cover" for an unforeseen departure or illness? Do they respond well to surprises in the marketplace? Start-ups require universal sacrifice, which can't be mandated very well.

6. *Recruitment of Talent*. Word-of-mouth is crucial for firms that can't afford big-time recruiters and ads, and whose jobs are often not even readily amenable to recruiting and advertising. Existing employees (and their families) tend to serve as vibrant and critical recruiting sources, minimizing cost, maximizing degree of talent available, and energizing the operation. When people want to come there to work, those already there feel a lot better about being there.

7. *An Important Forum.* We always are impressed by the Quaker
    meetings that still take place in many schools, wherein
    everyone sits in silence until someone feels like talking.
    Anyone may contribute, rebut, agree, or stay silent. We
    like that atmosphere in start-ups, too, where people in the
    relatively small group, in reality or virtually, can talk at any
    time and be heard. It serves as a human gyroscope that helps
    keep the company balanced.

Strategic commitment is an important element in *all* organizations. To deny that is to deny that finances or employee well-being
are important. But to admit it is to accept higher productivity, greater
motivation, and better sustainability.

AFTERWORD

Strategic Commitment is Essential in Volatile Economies

We've seen the benefits of strategic commitment globally in times of severe economic turmoil. Here are the benefits to organizations that strictly adhere to our premises during economic uncertainty and threat:

1. People stay focused on the goals, not the environment. There is a unifying strategic theme that supercedes outside conditions, which employees can't influence in any case. People remain positive and productive, rather than anxious, afraid and paralyzed.

2. The top team has a roadway to follow despite the storms all around. And when course corrections are needed, decisions remain contextual—in alignment with the strategy rather than in reaction to daily events. Strategic commitment provides the glue that allows people to change quickly without having the organization go off the rails.

3. The open, honest, trusting environment helps people quickly communicate problems, since the focus is on cause and not blame. The entire trust relationship aids immeasurably in quickly learning of problems and obstacles, and dealing with those rapidly and effectively.

4. The long term more easily takes precedence over short-term fluctuations. Organizations without commitment to a clearly

identifiable long-term strategy are those most likely to suffer a loss of will and hope.

5. Essential external relationships with customers, vendors, suppliers and credit agencies are strengthened through a clear obsession with responsiveness, service excellence, and quality of deliverables.

6. Market edge is improved through a calm, clear sense of confidence. Investors and customers—and potential employees—are encouraged by a sense of control and steadfast behavior.

7. Internal collaboration and innovation allows for increased productivity and performance in the face of scarce resources.

Lynn Pike, President of Capital One Bank since April 2007, is a great example of one executive leveraging strategic commitment to meet the challenges of today's unprecedented economic conditions—even in an industry currently under siege.

Late in 2008, with the financial world fully in the throes of unprecedented economic conditions, Lynn—who was already dealing with the typical integration strategies associated with Capital One's relatively recent entry-by-acquisition into core banking businesses—recognized the need for total alignment regarding priorities and leadership style.

Her team gathered to deal with the issues she believed would hinder them from being as effective as they could be in the face of the pressures the industry was under. They put context issues on the table, owned the areas where they had been individually or collectively acting in ways that may have impeded progress, and committed to a set of operating principles to guide their interactions. They scrutinized existing strategic plans for the upcoming year, and committed—100%—to each and every top-level priority and metric they would use to drive success.

"I strongly believed that the most important investment we could make was in ensuring that we as leaders were operating at a high level of sustainable trust and shared purpose. Not being on the same page about any of our priorities was an unacceptable position in this environment," says Lynn of her rationale for investing the time and effort to deal with these issues.

There are no guarantees of success, but the level of alignment and shared commitment Lynn and her team generated became a strong foundation for facing the turbulence everyone predicts will continue for the foreseeable future.

APPENDIX

Tips, Techniques, and Tools for Generating, Monitoring, and Addressing Setbacks Related to Strategic Commitment

The Strategic Commitment Scorecard: Finding Out Where You Stand (Chapter 2)

You may want to complete this scorecard yourself, then ask your key staff to complete it. Then you can compare notes. When comparing results with your colleagues, pay attention to areas of similarity and areas of differences, because they may be indicative of context issues as well.

If you would like additional copies of the scorecard, you may download the form or even complete it online at http://www.quantum performanceinc.com.

Scoring Scale
5 = We always do it; we're excellent.

4 = We mostly do it; we're good.

3 = We sometimes do it; we're average.

2 = We rarely do it, we're marginal.

1 = We never do it; we're bad at it.

There are twenty-eight statements in six areas. For each, place your score in the blank space provided.

I. Content Driver: Clarity

1. Every manager and employee in the organization can cite the mission and strategic goals of the organization. ____

2. Informal conversations are about how best to reach goals, not about confusion and cynicism about direction. ____

3. There are clear, symbiotic agendas and goals among departments, and not conflicting and self-defeating goals. ____

4. There are no conflicting priorities, internecine warfare, turf battles, reversals of decisions, and open refusals to cooperate. ____

II. Content Driver: Validity

5. People never excuse poor results by claiming the goals made no sense. ____

6. Surveys and feedback never indicate that employees feel uninvolved and are never asked for their opinions or input. ____

7. Commitment at meetings is matched by behavior and actions; there is no "lip service" agreement followed by inaction. ____

8. You never have to resort to punishment, coercion, or threat to create more support for initiatives and decisions. ____

9. People at all levels believe the organizational objectives and key initiatives make sense and are appropriately resourced. ____

III. Context Driver: Credibility

10. People believe management statements and communications, and there is no cynicism about trust and honesty. ____

11. Employees feel free to ask questions about what they are told and even to challenge things they hear. ____

12. People feel free to take risks and are not intent on minimizing their risk by covering their butts. ____

13. At the end of the day, real progress and movement can be empirically observed, as opposed to "going through the motions." ____

IV. Context Driver: Courage and Resolve

14. Leaders are seen to be in the front, taking risk and showing direction, taking blame but sharing credit. ____

15. "Whistle blowing" is encouraged, and there are no repercussions for identifying poor performance or bad implementation. ____

16. Decisions are made, communicated, and implemented with no vacillation, reexamination, or recrimination. ____

17. There is ready admission of mistakes, wrong direction, and error, and people seek cause, not blame. ____

18. Difficult and contentious issues are rapidly and effectively raised and addressed. ____

19. Management follows through on its commitments and proactively communicates when commitments must be modified. ____

V. Context Driver: Competence

20. People are seen to be promoted based on achievement, not tenure or low profile or political connection. ____

21. There is lateral communication, so there is no need to stay within hierarchies or silos; "turf" is subordinated to results. ____

22. Leaders earn the respect of their people and are   ____
accessible and visible, and while there may be
disagreement, there is always respect.

23. Employees go the "extra mile" for their   ____
leaders in terms of workload, hours, and
responsibilities, without resentment or
complaint.

VI. Context Driver: Care and Concern

24. Employees work with intensity for the corporate   ____
good, not personal goals, and do not demand
personal reward for every job.

25. Employees believe they are paid competitively,   ____
respected for their work, and promoted based on
merit.

26. Succession planning and career development   ____
plans are in place and are actively monitored by
senior management quarterly.

27. There is a mentor program, formal or informal, to   ____
help employees deal with challenges and provide
private support.

28. Employees feel valued and recognized for the   ____
work they do.

Scoring Results

115–140: You may just be at the cutting edge of strategic commitment, or you may be kidding yourself about how well you are doing. Very few organizations score this high.

98–114: You are doing well, with some room for improvement. Focus on those areas among the six where you are weakest for improvement.

70–97: You are in dangerous territory, because you got here by scoring "3" in all areas, which isn't very good. You might conclude that you are average. In fact, you probably are shining in one or two areas and doing poorly in the others.

50–69: You have major problems, and it's best to focus on one weak area at a time. We suggest, perhaps counterintuitively, that you begin with addressing context drivers to build credibility, and then focus on improving content drivers.

Below 50: Scores in this range indicate strategic weakness: high turnover, internecine warfare, political influence, coercion. These scores are typical of authoritarian organizations where employees are viewed as expenses, not assets.

Four Conversations That Will Tell You Where You Stand or Fall (Chapter 2)

If you would like a quick, anecdotal evaluation of where you stand (or fall) on strategic commitment, consider these four conversations.

Conversation One: With Employees

Talk to people throughout your organization, in person, by phone, and by e-mail. Don't interrogate them. Simply ask these questions:

- Are we making progress toward our strategic goals?
- How do you know?
- What are the obstacles in your way?
- How does your work change as we meet or miss goals?
- How often do you discuss these goals with your boss?
- What can I do to give you more help or direction?

If the responses you get from your employees indicate that they know the goals (e.g., "Well, our goal of greater market share in Europe is our toughest challenge because . . .), then you are off to a good start. But if they immediately resort to tactical responses and clearly do not know the strategic goals, you know you're in trouble. In our experience, most employees will talk about resource shortages, or too much work, or insufficient technology, which means they are focused on the day-to-day issues.

If employees tell you that they are uncertain of direction, don't have discussions about strategy, and aren't evaluated on any kind of strategic basis, at least they are thinking in the right terms, but they don't have the right support.

It won't hurt to put yourself in your employees' shoes every so often.

Hyatt Hotel executives were famous for taking a day or two a year and actually taking jobs as porters, desk clerks, and reservationists. This helped them truly understand what the employees were enduring. It also helped them understand to what degree tactics might be overwhelming strategy.

Conversation Two: With Direct Reports

After your conversations with employees, you'll have specific areas and executives with whom to have these conversations. Never believe that delegating everything and rarely "managing" direct reports is a perfect leadership style. You must be talking to these people regularly, and not just at meetings, in order to determine what their focus is on a routine basis.

If your executives are concerned about staffing problems, or the blood drive, or a new compensation system, or are fighting internecine wars, then they are not the exemplars you need for strategic commitment. In many, if not most, organizations, even senior executives become immersed in the daily grind. Find out if your executive team members spontaneously—without your prodding—raise strategic issues. Listen to them and then assess whether they are representing role models in both content and context drivers.

- Are they able to provide clarity and courage and demonstrate concern for their subordinates?

- Do they represent the competence that is needed to create commitment?

- Do your key people tend to talk about compliance measures or commitment initiatives?

- Are they trying to play traffic cop or catalyst?

Conversation Three: With Customers

Talk to your customers with the intent of determining whether your strategic (not merely tactical) initiatives are effective. The best approach is asking customers indirect questions.

For example, if you are curious about whether your strategic initiative is perceived as world-class in more than just your primary service area but also new ones introduced, you may want to inquire if your customers or clients are recommending you to others in those areas, and whether they plan to use you for a broader range of support. If your strategic initiative is to create longer-term contracts, ask whether the customer is considering such a relationship. Then ask why or why not.

Here are possible customer responses, bad to good:

- They are unaware of the initiative and intent.

- They heard something about it.

- They spoke to someone in your organization, but are confused.

- They have referred it for further study.

- They have a proposal on their desk that looks good to them.

- They have decided to do it.

Your clients' current perceptions will tell you a great deal about the effectiveness of your strategic commitment and will inform you as to whether it is strictly an insulated, internal initiative or is reaching the broader audience of clients and customers.

Conversation Four: With Yourself

If you are the leader possessing the traits we have discussed, then what do you have to do to improve and/or nurture strategic commitment? All of the other conversations—with employees, direct reports, and customers/clients—will give you intelligence about what you have to do.

What are you doing every day to support strategic commitment? You are the one who must make the tough decisions: Executives may not be on board, an initiative may have to be abandoned, you may have some unhappy news for the workforce or the board. Conversely, you are the primary cheerleader when goals are met, rewards are disbursed, and new initiatives are launched.

Working Back from a Future State: Getting "Unfrozen" (Chapter 3)

The process of getting an executive team to craft a bold, compelling future requires shedding the encumbrances of yesterday's and today's resource, capability, and cultural constraints. Without doing so, executives will unwittingly and unknowingly commit to a future state that is—at best—barely better or different from history and the present.

There are some very simple yet powerful ways to "unfreeze" people's relationship with history, all of which allow them to respect the past but not be handcuffed by it.

1. *Articles.* Ask people to write a one-or-two paragraph article (longer if they like—artistic license is appropriate in this case), dated two years' hence, which might appear in a well-respected industry publication. The article should capture the successes this group has enjoyed in beating competitors,

developing new products, increasing revenues, shifting their culture, or any of the other ways they have succeeded in winning over the previous two years. Invite people to read the articles aloud; we have repeatedly been struck by the creativity and commitment to success people have expressed during these readouts. With Gary Perlin's (Capital One's CFO) global finance team, they amazed themselves with the foresight they had had when revisiting the themes of these articles two years on, which not only validated their perspectives, but strengthened their resolve to pursue the mutual commitments they had made.

2. *Pictures.* Invite people to draw a picture of what the future will look like if the working environment *does not change.* While it can be enjoyable to speculate and brainstorm about how everyone would like the future to be, it is unusual for people to confront the more likely scenario—that without significant effort, things will stay exactly as they are. In a particularly striking situation, we asked the union and management leaders at a paper mill in Newfoundland—a facility that had been a chronic underperformer within the company portfolio and had a history of extremely adversarial labor relations—to draw pictures of the future sans change. The results were quite telling. One group of managers drew an image of a plane heading into the ground, with the management pilot and the unionized copilot pointing fingers at each other, one yelling "It's your fault" and the other, "No, it's your fault." A group of union leaders drew a picture of a cow and bull in a pasture. The cow (labeled "union") was drawn with a thought bubble saying, "Stay away from me," and the bull (labeled "managers") had a thought bubble saying, "I'm going to screw that cow." The refreshing honesty in the pictures, absent the blame, indignation, and insults so common in their day-to-day interactions, opened the door to a much more healthy and productive dialogue between the groups. Not surprisingly, better mill performance followed as well. Among the improvements: fewer grievances, fewer safety incidents, better operating efficiency, and the best

bottom-line results they had delivered in more than ten years.

3. *Broadway.* Give people a chance to portray the contrast between the past and present they are living in, and the desired future. They can express this in the form of a skit, song, or poem; they have complete artistic license. Within the Actuarial group at Prudential Financial, who among themselves joked of actuaries making accountants look like they have personalities, groups of actuaries spent no more than twenty minutes preparing past/future vignettes. The contrast was striking. Clearly evident among the entire group was the desire to build stronger partnerships with their line-of-business colleagues, share knowledge more effectively with each other across departments, and provide even more value to the company as a whole. All of these objectives had been part of Helen Galt's (Prudential's Chief Actuary and Chief Risk Officer) intentions for the group, but to see people generating their own expression of commitment to these objectives was a clear indication of their buy-in and full engagement. (Interestingly, one of the senior actuaries was later reported to have delivered a presentation on a fairly technical subject in the form of a rap song, breaking the mold and reputation of actuaries as unable to communicate technical information in a non-technical manner.)

There are undoubtedly numerous other creative ways to get people to think "outside the box," but these three methods seem to work well. The important principle is to not rush into listing all of the desirable attributes of the future without getting people's heads in the right place.

Crafting a Bold, Compelling Future State (Chapter 3)

The key questions that must be answered when articulating a strategic vision for an organization are spelled out in chapter 3. There are nuances to these questions that we capture here. We use the present tense to emphasize the urgent, promise-level commitment that helps cement people's relationship to the resulting statements:

When doing this, roll the clock forward to a specific point in time and answer these questions from then.

1. What do we uniquely provide, deliver, or impact?

   a. What is our unique capability and value to our customers (internal and external)?

   b. What kind of impact are we making?

   c. What differentiates us from other companies, areas, or functions?

   d. What businesses are we in and what services are we providing?

2. What is our distinct level of quality, performance, or delivery?

   a. What best describes our level of performance, style, or quality in terms of what we provide?

   b. What words are others using in describing our skills, offers, and competence?

   c. What benchmark are we known for? Are we "the best," "among the best," "known for something," "world-class," "number one," or something else?

3. What kind of team are we?

   a. What uniquely characterizes our internal culture and working dynamics?

   b. What do others say about our team dynamics?

   c. Are we cohesive? Innovative? Energized? Passionate? Relentless? Or something else?

Leadership Team Strengths and Weaknesses Assessment Instrument (Chapter 5)

This assessment instrument is intended for use by leadership team members to determine the current level of effectiveness of the behaviors of the *entire collective leadership team*. It is a very effective tool for determining the degree to which team behavior is consistent with the key leadership qualities and competencies required to generate strategic commitment.

Leadership Team Quantitative Assessment	
Category	Rating (1 = Low, 5 = High)

1. Orient around making a difference, rather than protecting egos and status.

    a. We are oriented around making a difference rather than promoting and protecting our own self-interests. ____

    b. We see ourselves as the means to our peers and our people's success, rather than them being the means to our success. ____

    c. We are obsessed with empowering others. ____

    d. We go out of our way to leave everyone energized and empowered in every interaction, even when the topic is uncomfortable. ____

    e. We deal with large and small issues from the big picture. ____

    f. We effectively balance individual and collective success. ____

    g. Our people acknowledge us for being oriented around making a difference rather than promoting and protecting our own egos and status. ____

2. Make the vision come alive in a meaningful way.

a. We are clear about, and present to others our vision, _____
commitment, and stand. We constantly make them
come alive for everyone.

b. We make all strategic, tactical, and operational _____
decisions based on our vision.

c. We refer to our vision in every meeting and _____
interaction.

3. Be authentic.

a. We are real, genuine, vulnerable, sincere, and _____
authentic in all communications, interactions, and
behaviors.

b. We have no hidden agendas. _____

c. We don't use our authority to avoid intimacy and _____
vulnerability.

d. We always express our true feelings. _____

e. We allow ourselves to be vulnerable. We don't _____
pretend we have it all together. We show our human
side.

f. We create intimacy with our team members. _____

g. Our people acknowledge us for being authentic in _____
all interactions and behaviors.

4. Operate with integrity.

a. We manage and keep all our commitments, no _____
matter how big or small.

b. We are always true to our values and principles. _____

c. Our people acknowledge us for our integrity. _____

5. Act with boldness and courage.

a. We have no issue acting and communicating _____
beyond our comfort zone.

  b. We keep pushing our own and others' envelope   ____
     about context and content challenges.

  c. We always challenge things from a place of   ____
     responsibility, not blame.

  d. We never settle for "we can't do that" or "this is as ____
     good as it gets."

  e. We constantly demand excellence of ourselves, each   ____
     other, and our teams.

  f. We operate with an "unstoppable" and   ____
     "uncircumstantial" (i.e., we don't let circumstances
     dishearten and stop us) winning mentality and
     spirit.

  g. We don't accept stories and excuses.   ____

6. *Have other's backs unconditionally.*
  a. We look out for other's backs unconditionally.   ____

  b. We feel others have our backs unconditionally.   ____

  c. We are really good at sharing and collaborating.   ____

  d. We really care about each other and feel others   ____
     genuinely care as well.

  e. Our people view us as role models for trust,   ____
     cohesion, and communication. We operate in their
     eyes as a single, united voice.

7. *Communicate openly and honestly.*
  a. We communicate openly, honestly, and   ____
     courageously.

  b. We leave all conversations complete (no holding back). ____

  c. We are always genuinely open.   ____

  d. We don't engage in any background conversations.   ____

  e. We hold each other to account and call each other   ____
     out when people don't live up to their commitments
     or values.

8. *Generate passion, energy, and enthusiasm.*

a. We generate passion, energy, enthusiasm, and   _____
   empowerment around us.

b. People are inspired by our energy and passion.   _____

9. *Build and empower leaders around us.*

a. We are constantly focused on developing, elevating,   _____
   and rewarding leaders. Building the next generation
   of leaders is one of the topics we spend our time on.

b. We invest sufficient time in mentoring, coaching, and   _____
   developing leaders. And we are very effective at it.

c. Our people acknowledge us for our obsession with   _____
   building and elevating leaders around us.

10. *Be committed to development and growth.*

a. We are obsessed with our own development and   _____
   growth.

b. We are constantly inspiring others to focus on their   _____
   development and growth.

c. We seek feedback and coaching, especially about   _____
   our own areas of weakness.

d. We are not defensive about feedback regarding our   _____
   leadership and performance gaps.

Instructions for Using the Assessment Instrument

1. Have each leadership team member fill out the assessment
   form and rate the overall team effectiveness on each of the
   ten leadership competencies and qualities. Make sure that
   members are assessing and rating the team as a whole, not
   individuals on the team.

2. Compile and graph the ratings based on the average of
   ratings given by all team members. An example is shown in
   the figure below.

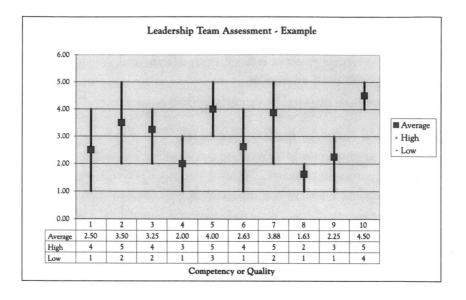

Leadership Team Assessment - Example

	1	2	3	4	5	6	7	8	9	10
Average	2.50	3.50	3.25	2.00	4.00	2.63	3.88	1.63	2.25	4.50
High	4	5	4	3	5	4	5	2	3	5
Low	1	2	2	1	3	1	2	1	1	4

Competency or Quality

3. Have a leadership team discussion around the collective views of the team strengths and weaknesses that addresses these areas:

a. What competency or quality do we believe we are strongest in, and why?

b. What competency or quality do we believe we are weakest in, and why?

c. On what competency or quality do we have the greatest divergence regarding our rating, and why?

d. What actions do we believe we need to take to either expand in the areas where we are strong or bolster those areas where we are weak?

e. Are there other constituents we should ask to assess our leadership strengths and weaknesses?

4. Agree to a time frame for conducting another quantitative assessment, and agree to owners for any actions from this meeting.

Leadership Strengths and Weaknesses
Assessment Recorder (Chapter 10)

Leaders also need to determine to what degree *individuals* in the organization are strong or weak in the ten key categories of assessment required to generate strategic commitment. Any assessment needs to take into account the individual's position in the company, but the categories for assessment should be the same.

Criteria for Assessment (for the full list of detailed questions for assessing each, see chapter 10, Figure 10-2):

- Orient around making a difference rather than protecting ego and status.
- Make the vision come alive in a meaningful way.
- Be authentic.
- Operate with integrity.
- Act with boldness and courage.
- Have other's backs unconditionally.
- Communicate openly and honestly.
- Generate passion, energy, and enthusiasm.
- Build and empower leaders around us.
- Be committed to development and growth.

The Process for Giving and Receiving Feedback

The process starts by having leadership team members give each other feedback on how well they are doing in terms of behaving consistently with these key leadership qualities and competencies. This exercise can be extremely powerful in building team openness, trust, and the ability to have deep, meaningful conversations about issues that often stay unspoken. You can facilitate the process yourself or use a skilled facilitator who can support leadership team members in being straight, honest, and direct in the giving of feedback, while at the same time remaining vulnerable and open to hearing honest feedback from their colleagues.

The giving and receiving of feedback (discussed in some detail in chapters 5 and 10) is about much more than the exchange of information from one person to another. It often requires individuals to dig deep within themselves to muster the courage to tell their colleagues if they are behaving in ways that will undermine the future to which they have collectively committed. We have seen executives express sentiments of resentment, betrayal, regret, anger, or remorse regarding events or incidents that have transpired. It is critical that everyone participating open not just their ears, but their hearts as well. We refer to it as "being wise not right!"

Instructions

Convene a meeting with the leadership team. If you do not have an outside facilitator, pick someone from the team to play that role. Then follow these steps:

Step One—Preparation. Using the leadership team strength and weaknesses assessment criteria (listed on the previous page), have each leadership team member record their findings on the form provided here, identifying and writing down the areas of strength and weakness for herself, as well as for each fellow team member. Have each team member list the names of all team members on the left column of the form, starting with their own name first. Pick the one or two prominent strengths and weaknesses for each individual and write them down in the respective columns; it is not necessary to rate each person on all ten criteria. Keep the list to one or two areas in each column. The preparation step will typically take fifteen to twenty minutes.

Name	Strengths	Weaknesses

Step Two—Self-Assessment. Once each person has filled out the form, have one person begin by sharing his assessment of his own strengths and weaknesses (starting with strengths). For example: "I believe I am strong at building leaders around me, and communicating openly and honestly. I believe I am weak at . . ."

Step Three—Feedback and Coaching. Once the first person has shared his self-assessment, the facilitator should select several team members to provide feedback and coaching to the first person. The facilitator should select members who work closely with the first person, but not those people he gets along best with. It does not need to be everyone on the leadership team, either, unless there is time to do so. The team members who have been asked for feedback should, in turn, give their assessments of the first person on both strengths and weaknesses, one at a time, making sure that the recipient understands the feedback and can own it. This does not mean the recipient of the feedback agrees with it, simply that he hears it, understands it, and has no questions about its meaning. The recipient can ask for clarification if necessary, but there is no rebutting or defending or arguing. The point of the conversation is to hear other people's reality regarding how one is doing as a leader. We also discourage note-taking while receiving feedback; we have found it to be more valuable for people to connect with each other by looking each other in the eye first. If they need to make a brief note afterward about something to follow up on, they may do so.

After receiving feedback from the few people who have been asked, there is then an opportunity for any other team members to add something, but only *if they feel it makes a difference*. This is not about piling on or making sure every voice is heard; it's about ensuring each team member has the full contribution of the team with respect to areas they are doing well in and areas where they need to improve.

Step Four—Repeating Steps Two and Three with All Members of the Team. Once the first person has completed the exercise, the next person should go, and so on until all team members have had their turn. We recommend against going sequentially around the table, as this will cause people to be worrying if their turn is next. Rather, proceed in a voluntary fashion, or by facilitator choice, with the exception that the most senior person in the group should take the last turn and should request feedback from each team member at the table.

Step Five—Completion. At the end of the exercise the floor should be opened to give people an opportunity to express their feelings about the value and impact of the exercise on their own personal development, as well as for the overall development of the team, especially in terms of how it elevated trust, partnership, and communication. We also recommend giving everyone a chance to express his or her respect and appreciation for each other's courage, generosity, commitment, and contribution. One way of doing this is to write everyone's name on pieces of paper and randomly distribute them to team members, ensuring no one receives her own name. Then have each person take a minute to acknowledge what that team member whose name they have received brings to the team in terms of commitment, dedication, professional competence, or some other quality unique to that individual.

We have conducted this exercise with thousands of teams in hundreds of companies and every time it has produced the following results:

1. A tremendous amount of personal leadership insight and development for all members.

2. An elevated sense of team spirit—specifically, people feeling that their peers care about them, are there "for them," and are committed to them.

3. An elevated orientation and competency within the team for open, honest, direct, and real communication, including about uncomfortable topics like feedback.

4. An elevated competency around providing feedback and coaching as a day-to-day norm.

It's invaluable. Try it.

INDEX

ABOUT THE AUTHORS

JOSH LEIBNER is a founding partner of Quantum Performance, Inc., a boutique management consulting firm with offices in Toronto and New Jersey. He has nearly twenty years' experience in organizational consulting within Global 1000 corporations and has designed, managed, and delivered business transformation projects involving direct interaction with more than 50,000 employees at all levels, from the boardroom to the shop floor, in North and South America, Europe, Africa, and the Far East. Josh has extensive experience in the design and facilitation of strategy development processes, executive team coaching and training, cultural values design and integration, and large-scale cultural change initiatives. He has worked within the financial services, telecommunications, automotive, food and beverage, pharmaceutical, entertainment, insurance, forest products, and biotechnology industries. His clients have included AT&T, Avaya, Campbell Soup, the Canadian Department of Corrections, Capital One Bank, Goodyear Rubber Chemicals, Guinness Brewing, Harris Bank, Lucent Technologies, Ogden Waste Management, Panavision, Pfizer, Prudential Insurance, Siemens Automotive, Technicolor Film Services, the United Way, and Zurich Financial Services. He lives in Bridgewater, New Jersey, with his son.

In addition to working with more than 50,000 people around the world on improving productivity and communication, GERSHON

MADER has managed an international training and consulting firm based in Israel where he worked closely with entrepreneurs and small businesses. After completing his military service in an elite commando combat unit, and retiring as a Captain, he continued to coach senior military officers and combat teams in high performance communication and team building. Gershon has extensive expertise and experience in coaching and consulting executives and managers to create bold and innovative strategies, as well as achieve dramatic improvements in individual and team productivity and performance. His 28 years of experience include designing and delivering large-scale business and cultural transformation initiatives, as well as coaching executive teams to become high performing teams. Gershon has consulted in a wide variety of industries, including telecommunications, technology, commercial real estate, financial services, manufacturing, entertainment, insurance, retail, and non-profits. His international experience includes working in, as well as with, Europe, Asia, North and South America, and the Middle East, at all levels of Fortune 500 and equivalent international organizations, from the boardroom to the shop floor, and with union executives and employees. Expert in his field, Gershon is a regular speaker at corporate events where he continuously receives outstanding accolades. In addition Gershon has been quoted in major publications including *Forbes*, plus he has co-published numerous articles on leadership and management in significant publications: "Chief Commitment Officer" in *HR Executive*; "Are You Executives Sabotaging Your Strategy?" in *Workforce Management*; and others. He is a founding partner of Quantum Performance, Inc., and lives in Toronto with his wife and three children.

ALAN WEISS is one of those rare people who can say he is a consultant, speaker, and author (and mean it). His consulting firm, Summit Consulting Group, Inc., has attracted clients such as Merck, Hewlett-Packard, GE, Mercedes-Benz, State Street Corporation, Times Mirror Group, The Federal Reserve, The New York Times

Corporation, and more than 500 other leading organizations. His speaking engagements typically include thirty keynote addresses a year at major conferences. He is a member of the National Speakers Association Hall of Fame. He is also a prolific writer of more than 500 published articles and twenty-seven books, including his best seller, *Million Dollar Consulting* (McGraw-Hill). His newest book is *The Global Consultant* (John Wiley and Sons). His books have been translated into German, Italian, Arabic, Spanish, Russian, and Chinese. In 2006, he was presented with the Lifetime Achievement Award of the American Press Institute (API), the first-ever awarded to a nonjournalist and one of only seven awarded in the sixty-year history of the API. He lives in East Greenwich, Rhode Island, with his wife of forty years. His two grown children are finally self-supporting.

*

Jason Leibner and Gershon Mader can be reached at: www.quantumperformanceinc.com.

Alan Weiss can be reached at: www.summitconsulting.com.

CPSIA information can be obtained at www.ICGtesting.com
Printed in the USA
BVOW03s1615011013

332565BV00006B/24/P